Oracle Fusion Middleware Patterns

Real-world composite applications using SOA, BPM, Enterprise 2.0, Business Intelligence, Identity Management, and Application Infrastructure

10 unique architecture patterns enabled by Oracle Fusion Middleware

Harish Gaur

Markus Zirn

PUBLISHING

BIRMINGHAM - MUMBAI

Oracle Fusion Middleware Patterns
Real-world composite applications using SOA, BPM, Enterprise 2.0, Business Intelligence, Identity Management, and Application Infrastructure

First published: September 2010

Production Reference: 1030910

Published by Packt Publishing Ltd.
32 Lincoln Road
Olton
Birmingham, B27 6PA, UK.

ISBN 978-1-847198-32-7

www.packtpub.com

Cover Image by Sandeep Babu (sandyjb@gmail.com)

Credits

Authors
Harish Gaur

Markus Zirn

Co-Authors
Mike Blackmore

Hamza Jahangir

Basheer Khan

Matjaz B. Juric

Sandeep Banerjie

Srikant Subramaniam

Nikhilesh Chitnis

Kiran Dattani

Milind Pandit

Mark Farabaugh

Sri Ayyeppen

Ross Sharman

Juliana Button

Matt Miller

Mark Simpson

Nam Doan-Huy

Yihong Xu

Narshimha Rao Kondapaka

Melody Wood

John Chung

Rex Thexton

Nishidhdha Shah

Acquisition Editor
James Lumsden

Development Editor
Dhwani Devater

Editorial Team Leader
Gagandeep Singh

Technical Editor
Vinodhan Nair

Indexer
Rekha Nair

Proofreader
Sandra Hopper

Graphics
Nilesh Mohite

Production Coordinator
Kruthika Bangera

Cover Work
Kruthika Bangera

Foreword

As you engage in enterprise architecture discussions with your customers, it becomes very evident that technology decisions are driven by business needs. And to solve these business needs, customers don't just look for products, they also look for implementation patterns to create solutions.

Unfortunately, building solutions has traditionally meant stitching together different technologies from different vendors. This causes issues because businesses innovate and change faster than ever before. Solutions now need to be delivered in six months rather than two years and once delivered, they must be flexible enough to withstand ongoing change. Clearly, building flexible solutions is hard when flexibility gets locked between a myriad of different technologies and tools.

With Oracle Fusion Middleware Suite 11*g*, we are revolutionizing the way new applications are created. Oracle is pioneering a new style of development—we provide an infrastructure that is complete and integrated. This integrated suite provides the best SOA, BI, Identity Management, Portal and Content Management tools, each engineered to work together. Earlier, developers had to build solutions programmed with thousand lines of code. Now, architects can compose (rather than build) a solution by combining multiple components of the Oracle Fusion Middleware Suite. This is exactly how Oracle has crafted its own next-generation Fusion Applications.

This book gives you an understanding of 10 unique patterns to compose solutions using multiple components of the Oracle Fusion Middleware stack. Every chapter highlights a unique pattern with its typical business drivers and what the architectural blueprint looks like. But, we wanted to make this real. That's why every pattern is backed up by a real-life customer scenario in which the specific pattern has been put into practice with the help of Oracle Fusion Middleware 11*g*.

We hope these field-tested patterns will inspire you to adopt the new "compose and configure" approach (rather than "build and program") as you create solutions to address your own business needs.

Hasan Rizvi, Senior Vice President, Oracle Fusion Middleware and Java

About the Authors

Harish Gaur is Director of Product Management for Fusion Middleware at Oracle. In this role, he works closely with strategic customers implementing Service-Oriented Architecture using Oracle SOA technology. Harish is the co-author of *BPEL Cookbook* from Packt Publishing. He holds an engineering degree in Computer Science and an MBA from Haas School of Business, UC Berkeley. Harish is an author and editor for this book.

Markus Zirn is Vice President of Product Management for Oracle Fusion Middleware. He is the editor of *BPEL Cookbook*, the author of several articles on SOA and related topics, and a frequent speaker at leading industry and analyst conferences. He holds a master's degree in Electrical Engineering from the University of Karlsruhe, Germany, the University of Southampton, U.K., and ESIEE, France.

About the Co-Authors

Mike Blackmore, Enterprise Architect at British Telecom, is responsible for leading the high-level technical relationship between BT and Oracle, engaging with BT and Oracle teams to make successful product and technology decisions.

Hamza Jahangir is a director of Enterprise Architecture at Oracle, and is co-author of Applied Oracle Security: Developing Secure Database and Middleware Environments (McGraw-Hill Osborne Media).

Basheer Khan is an Oracle ACE Director and President and Founder of Irvine, California-based Innowave Technology. Basheer was named Oracle Magazine's Integration Architect of the Year 2006 and Oracle Application Users Group (OAUG) Member of the Year in 2003.

Matjaz B. Juric holds a Ph.D. in computer and information science. He is the author/co-author of several SOA books, including *Business Process Driven SOA using BPMN and BPEL, Business Process Execution Language for Web Services* (English and French editions), *BPEL Cookbook*, and *SOA Approach to Integration*. He has consulted on several large SOA projects. Matjaz's latest book on *WS-BPEL 2.0 for SOA Composite Applications with Oracle SOA Suite 11g* is due out later in the summer.

Sandeep Banerjie is Senior Director of Product Management for Oracle Fusion Middleware. His responsibilities include developing and executing Fusion Middleware products and go-to-market strategies for Oracle and non-Oracle applications across all industries. Sandeep has IT experience of more than 17 years and is a frequent speaker on ERP, CRM, SCM, SOA, BPM, and Cloud Computing.

Srikant Subramaniam is a product manager for Oracle Fusion Middleware. He is responsible for enhancing and evangelizing best practices for the middleware platform as it relates to Oracle applications.

Nikhilesh Chitnis is Senior Sales Consultant for Oracle Fusion Middleware. He is responsible for positioning and demonstrating the value of Oracle's Middleware Suite of products to global customers. Nikhilesh has extensive expertise in the design, development, and implementation of software solutions across multiple industry domains.

Kiran Dattani is Director of Architecture Finance and Procurement for a major pharmaceutical company, where he is responsible for Global Architecture and Enterprise Integration projects. An accomplished speaker, he is a recognized expert in enterprise integration and supply chains in the life sciences and manufacturing industries.

Milind Pandit is an SOA Architect with Oracle Consulting Services, where he assists customers in deploying service-oriented architectures. He has 11 years' experience in software design, development, and implementation involving Enterprise Application Integration, J2EE, and Object-Oriented Analysis and Design.

Mark Farabaugh is a VP of IT at DJO in Vista, CA, leading DJO's multi-year program to consolidate all legacy ERP applications to a global single instance of Oracle EBS R12. Mark has more than 20 years of experience as an IT professional, and has focused on implementing Oracle enterprise applications such as ERP, BI, CRM, and FP&A for large multi-national corporations.

Sri Ayyeppen is the co-founder and CTO at Keste, an Oracle Platinum Technology Partner, where he is responsible for leading teams that deliver complex solutions with Oracle Applications, Technology, and Infrastructure. Sri was recently recognized as one of Oracle's Deputy CTOs for the year 2010.

Ross Sharman is the Technical Director for Knowledge Global, where his work on architecting and building the EMMA sustainability solution helped him to win the 2009 Green IT Architect Award from Oracle Magazine. Ross has an extensive background in technology and in electrical and electronic engineering, and has worked in large integration and Business Intelligence projects in Australia, the US, and Europe.

Juliana Button is Director of Product Management for Oracle Fusion Middleware. Since 1992, Juliana has held various technical and management positions in Oracle Corporation in Australia and at Oracle Headquarters in Redwood Shores. Her responsibilities include showcasing worldwide customer success with Oracle Application Grid products, as part of the Oracle Fusion Middleware Strategic Customer Program.

Matt Miller is Applications Director for Europe, Middle East, and Africa at GroupM. At the time of writing, he was Head of Business Analysts and Testing at Motability Operations and was also responsible for delivery of the Vehicle Remarketing technology project detailed in this book. Throughout his career Matt has worked in a wide variety or technical roles with several large media companies, including IPC Media, Associated Newspapers, and EMI Music.

Mark Simpson is an Oracle ACE Director specializing in SOA and Middleware. He leads the SOA technology practice for Griffiths Waite and is Solution Architect on Motability Operations Vehicle Remarketing SOA initiative. Mark has been an advisor on the deployment of SOA solutions at a host of leading organizations in the UK, and has led implementations based on Oracle Technology, including the first production Oracle SOA implementation in the UK and the first production Oracle Business Activity Monitoring implementation in the world.

Nam Doan-Huy is a Senior Manager in IT at Wind River Systems, a world leader in embedded and mobile software. In his role, Nam has responsibility for Oracle E-Business Suite architecture, Fusion Middleware including SOA, portals, Business Intelligence, and enterprise databases, supporting a wide range of business units. Prior to joining Wind River, Nam worked for a number of years in consulting as a technical lead for ERP implementations.

Yihong Xu, Wind River's Web Architect, has been with Wind River for 10 years. She started her career as a quality engineer and later switched to working with web technologies in 2003. As Web Architect, Yihong is responsible for developing web strategy, including translating business requirements into use cases, identifying and evaluating tools, selecting hardware and software platforms, and ensuring coherency across IT's heterogeneous web systems. Yihong has a Masters degree in Electrical Engineering.

Narshimha Rao Kondapaka is a Project Manager in IT and has been with Wind River for four years. Rao has more than 11 years of experience working with Oracle technologies and applications. He began his career as an Oracle Applications technical developer and switched to become an expert functional Business Analyst. Rao was recently promoted to Project Manager and played a key role in implementing the Online Support portal. Rao has a Master's degree in Computer Applications.

Melody Wood is a member of the Fusion Middleware Platform Product Management team, where she focuses on SOA and Web 2.0 customer deployment patterns. Melody joined Oracle in 1996, originally holding various partner management roles, where her increasing technical focus on Oracle product integrations across the database and middleware product stacks eventually led to her current role.

John Chung is Arcturus Realty Corporation's VP of IT and has over 10 years' experience in the real-estate industry, with diversified knowledge in technology and programming covering a broad range of languages and environments.

Rex Thexton is a managing director, and is a key leader of PricewaterhouseCoopers' Security and IdM practice in Oracle environments. Rex is an experienced IT professional with over 18 years of application development and IT management expertise. He has a proven track record for implementing strategic projects through a combination of effective relationship building with business leaders and technological aptitude. He was named and recognized as one of Oracle's Deputy CTOs, a select group of practitioners in North America.

Nishidhdha Shah works as senior consultant with PricewaterhouseCoopers. He has 10 years of experience in security and identity management. He holds CISSP and CISA credentials since 2006. He won ISC2 Cyber Security Awareness contest 2007 for his presentation on "Approach to security". Besides Schneider National, he also did a couple of large-scale OIM and ORM implementation in banking and retail.

Table of Contents

Preface

by Alex Andrianopoulos - Vice President of Fusion
Middleware Product Marketing at Oracle
Dain Hansen - Director of Fusion Middleware Product Marketing at Oracle

Enterprise Architecture is seldom simple enough to be built on a single technology—it generally encompasses a wide array of technologies, including SOA, Identity Management, Business Intelligence, Performance Management, Web 2.0, Content Management, BPM, Distributed Caching, Data Integration, and Application Servers.

What are the key business drivers where you need mix of a multiple technologies? What are the best practices (organizational as well as architectural) to meet enterprise needs? How do other organizations approach enterprise challenges that transcend technology and product boundaries? IT Leaders, CIOs, Enterprise Architects are searching for proof points.

This book is an attempt to answer these questions by illustrating 10 unique enterprise solution patterns to solve business needs in three specific areas—process improvement, business visibility, and collaboration and security. Each article will introduce a new pattern, along with an architectural overview of a real-world customer solution developed with Oracle Fusion Middleware.

Why Oracle Fusion Middleware?

All architecture patterns in this book are implemented with Oracle Fusion Middleware. Why is Oracle Fusion Middleware the right technology stack to compose agile and flexible solutions? That's because Oracle Fusion Middleware is built using the following unique design principles:

- **Complete**: There is no need to bring in multiple technologies from multiple vendors. This single stack addresses all middleware requirements.

- **Integrated**: All components within Fusion Middleware are built to work well with each other so you don't have to integrate them yourself. This translates into faster implementation and reduced operation costs.

- **Open**: All Fusion Middleware products are built using industry standards. They can not only integrate with each other, but also with existing IT infrastructure and applications with interoperability that goes beyond industry standards.

- **Best-of-breed**: Despite being integrated and complete, every product is best-of-breed bringing all the functionality you would expect from pure-play, niche products.

Let's take a quick look at different products within Oracle Fusion Middleware.

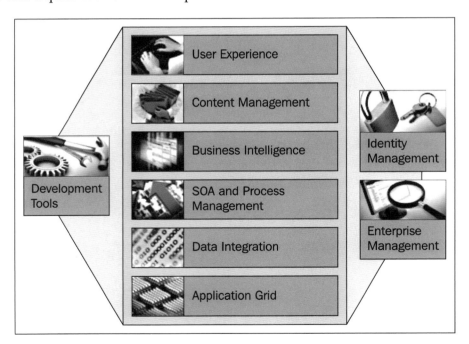

Application Infrastructure and Application Grid

Oracle's approach to application grid optimizes resources so applications get what they need, and when they need it, at a lower operational cost. Oracle WebLogic Suite 11*g*, the foundation of Application Grid, takes advantage of modern hardware and software architectures and delivers the highest performance, reliability, and agility at any scale. At the same time, Transaction Processing Monitors provide mainframe-class scale and performance for legacy systems in an open, distributed environment.

Data Integration

Oracle Data Integration provides a fully-unified solution for building, deploying, and managing real-time, data-centric architectures in an SOA, BI, and data warehouse environment. In addition, it combines all the elements of data integration (real-time data movement, transformation, synchronization, data quality, data management, and data services) to ensure that information is timely, accurate, and consistent across complex systems. This is achieved with the combination of Oracle Data Integrator and Oracle GoldenGate products (low-impact, real-time data integration).

Business Process Management and Service-Oriented Architecture

Oracle Fusion Middleware Business Process Management, Data Integration, and SOA capabilities provide a unified process platform for composing and managing adaptable and repeatable processes along with scaling out services. Process modeling, simulation, and standards-based execution accelerate the speed and accuracy of development, while Data Integration and SOA Governance provide information and service-level agreement clarity. Oracle SOA Suite 11*g* delivers a complete, integrated, best-of-breed technology foundation for building next generation business applications.

Business Intelligence and Strategic Decision-Support

Oracle Business Intelligence Enterprise Edition Plus and Data Integration capabilities enhance the quality and accuracy of business analysis across data sources and speed the delivery of information to those who need it. Pre-built business intelligence applications and Enterprise Performance Management capabilities help enhance the quality and timeliness of strategic business decisions — from the executive suite to individual lines of business such as manufacturing, sales, and human resources.

Enterprise Portals, Content Management, and Team Collaboration

Oracle's Fusion Middleware Enterprise 2.0 Portal and Content Management solutions create rich connections among your people, processes, information, and applications for greater productivity and cost savings. Oracle offers a comprehensive strategy based on choice, innovation, and information excellence, whether you're consolidating portals, embracing social networking technologies for improved productivity, or *going green* with paper-based processes. Oracle WebCenter Suite 11*g* is a complete, open enterprise portal platform for creating enterprise portals, social and composite applications, and internet and extranet websites.

Identity Management

Significantly reducing the overhead costs of security and administration along with protecting sensitive business information, Oracle Fusion Middleware Identity Management solutions automate user provisioning and deprovisioning and provide single sign-on capabilities for information security and user productivity. A unique, application-centric approach delivers vast improvements in the speed of compliance and e-discovery exercises, worker productivity, and reduced business risk. Oracle Identity Management 11*g* is a fully-integrated suite that provides the foundation for Oracle's Service-Oriented Security strategy.

Oracle Fusion Middleware maximizes value for your Oracle applications

Successfully managing challenges such as integrating applications, extending application capabilities, securing and managing identities across applications, managing unstructured information around applications, and business intelligence all require a strong technology platform. Customers are experiencing greater business value, lower costs, and faster time-to-value by extending and enhancing their enterprise applications with Oracle Fusion Middleware.

What this book covers

Chapter 1 discusses a new approach to application development and enterprise architecture—Fusion development and Oracle Enterprise Architecture. These principles lay the foundation of any agile and flexible solution IT needs to deliver to the business. Rest of the book is conceptually divided into three sections dedicated for solutions in three areas—process improvement, business visibility and collaboration, and security.

Chapter 1, Building Agile Applications using Fusion Development and Oracle Enterprise Architecture Principles, introduces the concept of Fusion development and Oracle Enterprise Architecture (OEA). These principles serve as a guideline to create flexible and agile solutions. This chapter will demonstrate how British Telecom defined Universal Application Framework using OEA and Fusion Middleware technologies. UniApp framework helped BT to drive consolidation of 46 different applications down to one and implement application development standardization. This chapter also highlights how Pardee Homes, major home builder in California, USA, adopted the Fusion Development approach to assemble its solution, leveraging components of Oracle Fusion Middleware, including Oracle BPA Suite, Oracle BPEL Process Manager, Oracle Web Services Manager, Oracle ADF, and Oracle Application Server.

Section 1: Process Improvement

Businesses often grapple with questions like "How do I improve efficiencies in my core business processes and make it more agile?", "How can I improve the response time of my SOA applications while minimizing hardware costs?", or "How do I extend the value of my ERP applications?". Unfortunately, there is lack of integrated tools to handle entire process lifecycle—modeling, integration, execution, management, and monitoring of business processes. No standardization in application development. Performance of composite applications is generally an after-thought. Next three chapters provide solution patterns to answer these questions through process improvement approach.

Chapter 2, Process-driven SOA Development, highlights how SOA can help IT align with key business processes. SOA reduces the semantic gap between IT and business by introducing a development model that aligns the IT development cycle with the business process lifecycle. This chapter introduces reader to organizational and technical aspects of SOA development. It then describes how Elektro Slovenija, Slovenia's state-owned power distribution company, transformed its procurement process using Oracle BPA and Oracle SOA Suite.

Chapter 3, Code-free Application Extensions and Integrations, deals with the most common problem we see in our ERP install base—how do I extend my ERP applications? Fusion Middleware plays a critical role here. This chapter illustrates how you can use SOA, BPM, Web 2.0, and BI to extend and integrate Oracle applications without writing a single line of code. The approach makes these modifications simple, quick to implement, and easy to maintain/upgrade. It offers an innovative and practical solution to radically change the economics of running Oracle applications.

Chapter 4, Data Tier Caching for SOA Performance, is all about improving the performance of composite SOA applications. Performance/scalability issues have grown to be the one of the topmost concerns when building an SOA application. This chapter introduces a new architecture pattern—boosting SOA performance with distributed caching. It discussed how a mid-tier caching strategy can inject high performance into data services as part of a SOA. It also illustrates the approach a major pharmaceutical company took to improve the performance of a composite application using an Oracle Coherence Grid solution with Oracle SOA Suite.

Section 2: Business Visibility

Business constantly struggle with questions like "How do I make sound business decisions with disconnected data?" or "How can I measure my KPIs and improve them in real-time?". Challenge is that there is no unified platform available in the market to handle "what-if" and "how" analysis. BI dashboards are traditionally not actionable by business users and there is no real-time intelligence for on-the-fly decision making. Next three chapters provide user with solution patterns to achieve business visibility.

Chapter 5, Integrated Real-time Intelligence with Oracle's WebCenter, Coherence, and Business Activity Monitoring, describes reference architecture for contextual, real-time business insight that uses BAM and E2.0 to combine information management and analytics in the same context and transaction. A combination of BI and E2.0 allows us to combine information management and analytics in the same context and transaction. Using DJO, a leading global provider of high-quality orthopedic devices as an example, this chapter walks through a real-life example of how this is accomplished using Oracle WebCenter, Oracle Business Activity Monitoring, and Oracle Coherence.

Chapter 6, Achieving Business Insight by Integrating Relational and Multi-dimensional Data, tackles how organizations need to simultaneously address situational questions ("What"), and forward-looking questions ("How") as part of their every day organizational reporting and planning needs. Through the use of a real-world example, this article highlights a compelling business need to integrate relational and multi-dimensional data. We will discuss how the Australia-based Knowledge Global has used the combined power of Oracle BIEE, Oracle Essbase and Oracle Data Integrator to build a carbon/energy monitoring and measurement application.

In *Chapter 7, Building Intelligent Processes with Insight-driven Agility,* discusses how convergence of BI and SOA allows organizations to become agile. Business SOA and BI are natural partners for a changing organization. Processes that are supported by SOA allow the organization to directly execute the business model and better support business change; BI provides measures that inform decisions for strategic and tactical change within an organization. Combining SOA with BI allows you to act on those measures, changing processes, services, and rules to target identified improvement goals. In this chapter, we will show how Motability Operations is creating a platform to monitor and improve vehicle remarketing efforts across multiple channels using Oracle OBIEE, Oracle BPEL PM, and Oracle Business Rules.

Section 3: Collaboration and Security

Last section deals with collaboration and security. If you are grappling with issues like "How do I open up to new communities and channels without compromising my organization's brand, intellectual property, and customer data?" , "How do I enable customer self- service in a collaborative environment?", or "How can I automate employee onboarding to achieve compliance?", then you might have realized that there is no effective way to handle collaboration across different contributors. Data could be widely dispersed in structured (database) or unstructured (e-mail, chats, VOIP, and others) format. There is a need for appropriate checks and balances to maintain security and privacy, but tools are ineffective in doing so. Next three chapters provide solution patterns to address business issues around collaboration and security.

Chapter 8, Building Enterprise 2.0 Applications, examines the key building blocks of Enterprise 2.0 architectures and then outlines important integration considerations for building an Enterprise 2.0 application. The fundamental capabilities of any rich Enterprise 2.0 requires the combination of content management, a Web 2.0 framework, security, and integration with enterprise applications. This chapter also illustrates how Wind River, a software device optimization company, leveraged Oracle WebCenter and Oracle Enterprise Content Management platform to revamp its online customer support portal.

Chapter 9, Automating Enterprise Reporting with WebCenter, SOA, and Oracle Business Intelligence Publisher, explains how to optimize enterprise reporting within a company. It explains how to build an automated reporting platform with SOA, an enterprise reporting tool, and a portal. It then walks through a real-life example of how Arcturus, a leading real estate services company, built a property management reporting solution using Oracle Business Intelligence (BI) Publisher, Oracle SOA Suite, and Oracle WebCenter.

Chapter 10, A Role-based Approach to Automated Provisioning and Personalized Portal, demonstrates how an organization can take a role-based approach to automate provisioning and personalize a portal. The solution should include four key components: a provisioning platform, a role management platform, an access management platform, and a portal. The chapter explores how Schneider National, a multinational trucking company, successfully automated employee on-boarding and personalized its intranet portal using Oracle Role Manager (ORM), Oracle Identity Manager (OIM), and Oracle WebCenter.

Who this book is for

This book is intended for IT professionals, architects, managers, and project managers who are responsible for planning, designing, providing, and operating software solutions to meet business needs.

Conventions

In this book, you will find a number of styles of text that distinguish between different kinds of information. Here are some examples of these styles, and an explanation of their meaning.

Code words in text are shown as follows: "If the value for this field is set to `true`, then the content is accessible only to employees".

A block of code is set as follows:

```
<attachment>
  <mimeType>application/pdf</mimeType>
  <name>July 2010 Bank Statement & outstanding chq List 360
    Laurier.pdf</name>
  <updatedBy>acardenas</updatedBy>
  <taskId>32687d765b75fb16:3b24ea99:128ee025f4d:2840</taskId>
  <version>3</version>
</attachment>
```

When we wish to draw your attention to a particular part of a code block, the relevant lines or items are set in bold:

```
<local-scheme>
  <scheme-ref>default-eviction</scheme-ref>
  <!-- Eviction policy set to LRU, so that least recently used cache
    data is evicted to make room for new cache -->
  <eviction-policy>LRU</eviction-policy>
  <high-units>0</high-units>
  <!--Expiry set to 0, so that the cached data never expires. -->
  <expiry-delay>0</expiry-delay>
</local-scheme>
```

New terms and **important words** are shown in bold. Words that you see on the screen, in menus or dialog boxes for example, appear in the text like this: "Clicking on **Submit new travel request** presents a data entry form to submit a travel authorization request".

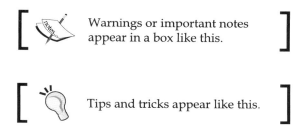

> Warnings or important notes appear in a box like this.

> Tips and tricks appear like this.

Reader feedback

Feedback from our readers is always welcome. Let us know what you think about this book—what you liked or may have disliked. Reader feedback is important for us to develop titles that you really get the most out of.

To send us general feedback, simply send an e-mail to feedback@packtpub.com, and mention the book title via the subject of your message.

If there is a book that you need and would like to see us publish, please send us a note in the **SUGGEST A TITLE** form on www.packtpub.com or e-mail suggest@packtpub.com.

If there is a topic that you have expertise in and you are interested in either writing or contributing to a book, see our author guide on www.packtpub.com/authors.

Customer support

Now that you are the proud owner of a Packt book, we have a number of things to help you to get the most from your purchase.

> **Downloading the example code for this book**
>
> You can download the example code files for all Packt books you have purchased from your account at http://www.PacktPub.com. If you purchased this book elsewhere, you can visit http://www.PacktPub.com/support and register to have the files e-mailed directly to you.

Errata

Although we have taken every care to ensure the accuracy of our content, mistakes do happen. If you find a mistake in one of our books—maybe a mistake in the text or the code—we would be grateful if you would report this to us. By doing so, you can save other readers from frustration and help us improve subsequent versions of this book. If you find any errata, please report them by visiting http://www.packtpub.com/support, selecting your book, clicking on the **errata submission form** link, and entering the details of your errata. Once your errata are verified, your submission will be accepted and the errata will be uploaded on our website, or added to any list of existing errata, under the Errata section of that title. Any existing errata can be viewed by selecting your title from http://www.packtpub.com/support.

Piracy

Piracy of copyright material on the Internet is an ongoing problem across all media. At Packt, we take the protection of our copyright and licenses very seriously. If you come across any illegal copies of our works, in any form, on the Internet, please provide us with the location address or website name immediately so that we can pursue a remedy.

Please contact us at copyright@packtpub.com with a link to the suspected pirated material.

We appreciate your help in protecting our authors, and our ability to bring you valuable content.

Questions

You can contact us at questions@packtpub.com if you are having a problem with any aspect of the book, and we will do our best to address it.

1
Building Agile Applications using Fusion Development and Oracle Enterprise Architecture Principles

by Mike Blackmore, Hamza Jahangir, Harish Gaur, and Basheer Khan

According to Gartner Research, medium- to large-scale IT organizations spend, on an average, not more than 20 percent of their budget on new projects. That seems like a very low number given the speed at which business is changing. From new social media-based marketing techniques to open Web 2.0-style collaboration for customer service, to modern predictive analytics, business seems to be on a march towards fundamental transformation, while the underlying IT always seems to be catching up. So, why do we spend such a small proportion of the IT budget on innovating and modernizing to meet the demands of the business?

The problem is that keeping the lights on in our IT organizations is becoming an increasing cost to the business and gobbling up a larger chunk of the IT budget every year. If IT is to keep pace with the level of demand for information from the business, the costs will likely grow at the same pace or faster, unless the enterprise implements a fundamentally new approach to managing IT applications and systems.

In this chapter we introduce two approaches—Fusion Development (an application development process) and Oracle Enterprise Architecture (an architecture development framework and process) for governing the way IT organizations manage changes to business demands and requirements without ripping and replacing the existing architecture and technology foundation. This chapter discusses Fusion Development and Oracle Enterprise Architecture application at two companies—British Telecom (BT) and Pardee Homes.

Enterprise application development challenges

Over the past decade, most enterprises have responded to information demands by procuring or developing new applications without much consideration of the underlying technology foundation. This is understandable behavior given that the immediate priority was to deliver discrete functions, such as billing and human resources, delivered by packaged or home-grown applications. Today, as those types of **Enterprise Resource Planning** (**ERP**) systems are becoming commoditized, businesses are starting to harness value by cross-referencing and correlating data from multiple systems to gain new insight about the business. In Web 2.0 parlance this is referred to as a *mash-up*, in which data from many sources is combined to deliver a rich, composite view to the business user. Increasingly, this is moving from a nice-to-have feature in our enterprise applications to one that is absolutely required to remain competitive in almost all areas of the business. However, the transition to that form of composite enterprise application architecture is challenging, mainly for the following reasons:

- Existing applications were not meant to interact technologically or semantically (that is, no canonical or semantic data model for business data)

- No centralized integration process or platform for applications to exchange and share the necessary data

- Hard to manage security and privacy of sensitive business data

Another unique aspect of these kinds of composite applications is that they go through much faster lifecycles; the speed of requirement change is getting faster as the overall speed of change increases around business strategies and processes. This necessitates more frequent additions and changes to the application, which traditional software development processes are not able to handle very well. The modern enterprise application development needs to be much more responsive and iterative in nature if it is to deliver features on time to the business. As a result, with the new application architecture, driven by fusing information from disparate data sources, IT must also take a fundamentally new approach to its application development capabilities. It must be able to deliver modern enterprise applications faster and more cost-effectively and prevent a cost explosion as your need for information continues to grow. This new approach must be comprehensive and span all the way from architecture development to implementation to change management.

Fusion development

Before we get into Fusion development and the **Oracle Enterprise Architecture Framework (OEAF)**, let's consider a modern apartment complex in terms of how it is designed. Units have a different number of bedrooms, different interior designs to fit the owners' needs, and yet follow a common architecture for common services like water, electricity, and gas. The modern IT organization is similar in the sense that while individual lines of business and departments might be asking for different types of applications, systems, and data, there needs to exist a common architecture that provides a framework upon which new applications can be built easily and quickly. This framework should reuse a lot of common patterns and infrastructure services, such as information storage, security, monitoring, and so on. If we are able to reuse these basic services repeatedly, the focus for application development can transition from coding applications to composing applications from existing services.

This is the fundamental approach of Fusion development—solutions are assembled, not written. Solutions are built by assembling services together, and in the process, they transcend disparate technology boundaries. Oracle is pioneering this new style of development. Oracle Fusion Middleware is making this happen here at Oracle. Oracle Fusion Middleware is the convergence layer for existing and future Fusion applications and services. Fusion applications and services are built on Fusion Middleware infrastructure and utilize diverse technologies, including **Service-Oriented Architecture (SOA)**, **Business Intelligence (BI)**, Identity Management, Enterprise Content Management, Coherence, **Business Process Management (BPM)**, **Complex Event Processing (CEP)**, and Application Servers.

In principle, Fusion Development is very similar to **Extreme Programming** and **iterative development**, and is heavily influenced by SOA. The focus is on applications that can be quickly built and easily managed. The following figure illustrates the key steps to building such an application using the Fusion Development approach:

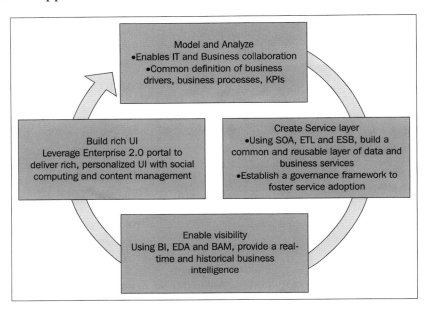

Starting at the top:

- **Model and Analyze**: Having a common understanding of how the business functions, which applications and people are involved, and the key business drivers is an essential element of Fusion development. This requires bringing key business stakeholders together with their IT counterparts to collaborate and iron out any differences in understanding. This results in well-defined process models, schemas, and **Key Performance Indicators** (**KPI**) that eliminate any concerns that the business requires, but IT can't deliver (Refer to *Chapter 2, Process-Driven SOA Development*).

- **Create Service Layer**: Services play a very important role in the concept of assembling applications. In this step, we build a portfolio of reusable data, business, and application services. These become the building blocks for composing new applications with the utmost speed and flexibility (Refer to *Chapter 3, Code-free Application Extensions and Integrations* and *Chapter 4, Data Tier Caching for SOA Performance*).

- **Enable Visibility**: Business decisions are driven by insight. These insights are delivered to the business user, in this step, using BI, Event-driven Architecture, Essbase, and BAM. Using real-time and historical intelligence, business users can monitor the health of a business and take corrective actions (Refer to *Chapter 6, Achieving Business Insight by Integrating Relational and Multi-dimensional Data* and *Chapter 7, Building Intelligent Processes with Insight-driven Agility*).

- **Build Rich UI**: In this step, users get a personalized view of their dashboard in a rich, Web 2.0 environment. It brings together content, workflow, and dashboards and offers a seamless UI experience (Refer to *Chapter 5, Integrated Real-time Intelligence Using Oracle WebCenter, Oracle Coherence, and Oracle Business Activity Monitoring* and *Chapter 8, Building Enterprise 2.0 Applications*).

Oracle Enterprise Architecture

Since Fusion Development enables rapid application development through composition instead of coding, the barriers for an enterprise to make changes are lowered. But this isn't necessarily always a good thing for IT organizations. Rapid application development and changes can unfortunately foster rapid decision-making without a full understanding or assessment of the true impact of those decisions. Just because we can quickly change doesn't necessarily mean we can always recover from big mistakes. In fact, rapid and extreme programming techniques can sometimes expedite the process of failure if not properly governed by a common vision and a well thought-out decision-making framework.

The **Oracle Enterprise Architecture Framework (OEAF)** and **Oracle Architecture Development Process (OADP)** provide a decision-making framework that can be used with Fusion development to provide IT organizations with a mechanism to make fast decisions that align with a central vision and direction. The point of using OEAF and OADP is not to get in the way of agile development, but steer it in a way that maximizes the value of IT to the business.

The OEAF is an EA framework (similar to TOGAF and Zachman), but specialized to realize three key principles:

- **Simple and practical**: In other words, this is not an architecture modeling exercise but a practice to get to tangible business value

- **Start with the business**: The OEAF is an architectural framework that always starts the conversation from the point of view of the business and what it is trying to achieve

- **Leverage existing assets**: The OEAF comes with a library of the latest reference models, best practices, and reference architectures from Oracle and the industry to expedite the process of deciding on the best approaches for your enterprise

The OEAF is organized into the architectural views illustrated in the following figure:

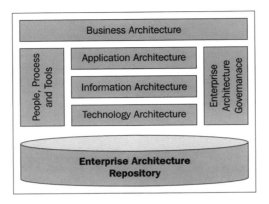

The OADP is a companion to the OEAF, providing it with some prescriptive guidance on the sequence of decisions that should be made before we start developing applications and other IT capabilities. The process can be leveraged by senior IT management to lay a foundation for all day-to-day operational decisions. In a very simplistic view, OADP provides a process for defining the vision for the future-state of IT and a systematic way to arrive at that future state through appropriate architecture and IT governance methods. At a high level, the OADP process is broken into phases, as illustrated in the following figure:

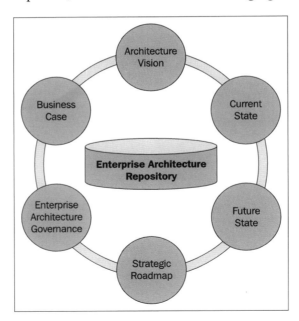

OADP is a highly collaborative and iterative process where assumptions are constantly refined and tested to ensure that the IT organization is operating as effectively as possible to deliver requirements defined by the business. Also, OADP advocates a mindset based on principles and performance metrics to manage IT projects. If those principles and performance metrics are clearly articulated and understood by the organization, there is no need to micromanage projects. This concept is exemplified in the British Telecom use case described in the next section, in which the Chief Architect managed the entire British Telecom IT organization using 12 simple rules.

IT rationalization at British Telecom Property Group

British Telecom is a global corporation that is more than 100 years old, operating in over 170 countries worldwide, with more than 100,000 employees. British Telecom's Group arm handles the procurement of all BT goods and services, managing over 10,000 properties and running 50,000 vehicles. Over 150,000 people require daily access to 10,000+ buildings in which to work and meet.

The BT Property system's estate had grown organically through first and second generation web applications and stood at 46 systems. These systems utilized a wide variety of application and database technologies, including ColdFusion, ASP, .NET, J2EE, Oracle 8i, Oracle 9i, SQL Server, and MS Access.

Because of this organic system growth, business processes sat in fragments of code in web pages, as stored procedures in databases, as cells in spreadsheets, and all too often just in peoples' heads. For customers, these issues manifested a very poor user experience, plagued by low systems reliability, low availability, and thus reduced utilization of the BT Property estate. The effect on the actual property estate was tangible, as building maintenance problems went unreported and unresolved.

This state of affairs was recognized by both BT Design (the BT IT services delivery organization) and BT Group Property (the customer). BT's application management costs were increasing sharply and, at the same time, there was a corresponding decrease in trust in an important BT function. BT decided to rationalize their systems by putting together an enterprise architecture framework and standardizing the application development.

BT UniApp Framework

BT Procurement worked with BT Enterprise IT. BT Procurement's strategy was systems rationalization, service orientation, and agile delivery, while delivering a radically improved but lower-cost service to the customer. The new architecture of the UniApp is designed to break away from the dictates of IT fashion, to exploit BT's wider software investments, and become a foundation for reducing IT expenditure.

The new UniApp architecture provides BT's business support operations with a standards-based, resilient, and scalable platform from which to deliver IT services to the wider business. Most importantly, it provides a sustainable platform that can accommodate the broadest range of human and automated business processes and workflows within its scope (BT Real Estate in the first instance, but applicable to any other niche business support operation without a dedicated vendor-supported software stack). BT put together the Fusion Middleware-based UniApp Framework to provide a rapid, business process-led development environment, methodology, and delivery capability to solve this critical business problem. The UniApp Framework is built along the same principles as prescribed by OEAF.

BT laid out the golden rules. Take a look how they compare with OEAF principles described previously:

OEAF principle	BT UniApp golden Rule
Simple	Keep it simple! There are three layers to the UniApp—Where the data is stored, how it gets there, and what people need to see.
	The Database WILL use a Single Schema.
	There will be ONE Schema per UniApp Platform.
	A single Security model will apply to each UniApp Platform.
Start With Business	These are Platforms for innovation, able to bring SaaS to the BT Group community and transform expectations of its IT systems. Innovate with them!
Leverage Existing Assets	UniApp will ONLY be used where customization of a COTS ORACLE package would become intrusive and provide a poor user experience.
	We will NOT duplicate functionality provided by other Platforms, including the EMP integration Architecture.

A quick look inside the UniApp Framework

The BT UniApp is a three-layered architecture separating the user experience/page flow from the workflow and data layers. The user experience is based on the Oracle Application Development Framework, presented to the user by the Oracle WebCenter Framework. The workflow element is handled by Oracle SOA Suite for both human (BPEL for People) and systems workflow and integration. The database layer is, as one would expect, entirely abstracted from the user, although with very strong governance from a design and development perspective. This provides BT with a rich, comprehensive, and robust environment in which to design, build, and deploy Web 2.0 applications to meet requirements in the BT Enterprise Management space, where no off-the-shelf Oracle ERP applications are available (see the following figure).

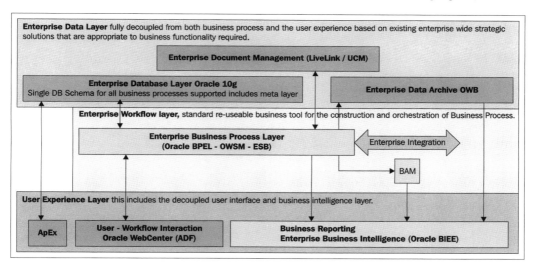

BT was able to wrap this approach in a rigorous governance structure and process that allowed the organization to evaluate the applicability of the solution to a given problem. That process ensures that Oracle ERP applications are evaluated first, eliminating duplication of functionality.

The principles of the UniApp (which are maintained through the aforementioned governance process) stress the need to leverage the core native capabilities of the Oracle products that make up the components of the UniApp. When required functionality cannot be met with these core products, and a compromise is required, the compromise will always comply with the architectural principles set out for the UniApp. In practice, the need for user stories based on such compromises rarely occurs; the agile process reveals what the user really wants. This stands in sharp contrast to the previous approach, in which users stated not only what functionality they wanted, but also how the functionality would be implemented. The agile approach removes preconceptions from the design process and allows the capabilities of the components to be demonstrated. The long-term cost reduction benefits to the organization from maintaining a standards-based approach outweigh the short-term needs of an individual delivery. The aim is composition not customization.

Benefits realized by British Telecom

BT's solution took about five months to build, using an agile methodology implemented by a team of four onshore and 10 off-shore developers. The BT Buildings website records over 40,000 hits per day, and the solution supports over 40 key BT Property processes, including those related to critical safety and security functions.

Process improvement at Pardee Homes

Now let's take a look at another example in which principles of Fusion development were put into practice.

Pardee Homes, a major home builder in California, has been building award-winning homes and neighborhoods for more than 87 years. To support their business, Pardee Homes continues to innovate and strengthen their IT system by investing in the latest and greatest technologies.

The company chose to overhaul its entire IT system with an upgraded ERP system, and new sales, options, warranty, and scheduling systems. The overhaul also included enabling seven disparate systems to talk to each other in real time, supporting about twenty cross-application transaction types. Pardee's requirements included support for over a thousand concurrent transactions while guaranteeing a reliable message delivery. Also required was the ability to view the status of these transactions across various applications, with an easy recovery process in case of delivery errors.

Pardee Homes also wanted to automate its purchase order and invoice approval process. Automated document scanning and approval workflow initiation were to be included, providing users with task lists and visibility into the documents that needed their approval.

Overall, the solution had to be flexible and able to accommodate future systems with the minimal effort. Utilizing industry's leading technologies and methodologies was crucial to this solution in order to allow Pardee Homes to maintain its leadership in the home-building industry.

Four steps to Fusion development

Pardee Homes adopted the Fusion development approach to assemble its solution, leveraging components of Oracle Fusion Middleware, including Oracle BPA Suite, Oracle BPEL Process Manager, Oracle Web Services Manager, Oracle ADF, and Oracle Application Server:

1. **Model and analyze**: At a very early stage, Pardee Homes invited key business stakeholders to partner with IT team members to map out their existing enterprise-wide processes using Oracle BPA Suite, shifting the focus and concentration to process improvement. This facilitated process alignment with corporate goals and strategy, establishing a corporate-wide framework and repository of processes for land development, purchasing, finance, accounting, sales, and options. This approach enhanced employee awareness and the visibility of business processes, promoting business process analysis, optimization, and improvement. It also supported business process transformation and seamless integration with technology by leveraging Oracle BPEL for process execution.

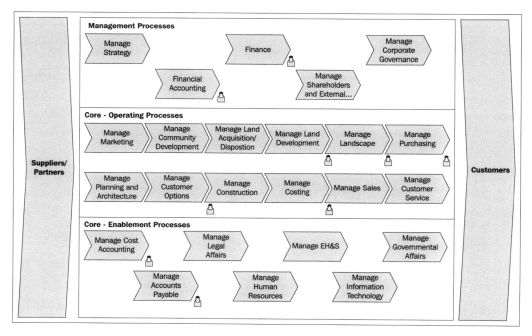

2. **Create Service Layer**: The next step was to design and develop a layer of reusable services to enable integration and workflow automation. This involved standardizing the entities used across the enterprise, identifying the business events in each system, and building the services that would be required in each system. This layer also included the ability to secure the services, and leveraged SOA governance to maintain and organize the SOA artifacts. Pardee Homes chose to use the **Oracle Application Integration Architecture** (**AIA**) methodology to identity Enterprise Business Objects, Enterprise Business Services, and Enterprise Business Flows. Oracle BPEL served as the Enterprise glue, listening to Business Events across systems and then routing the messages to the target systems. Oracle Web Services Manager provided the pluggable security layer around each system service, allowing each service call to be authenticated and callable only from BPEL. The SOA-based interaction with other components of the solution provided the benefits that come with an SOA-based environment in terms of maintenance, flexibility, scalability, and reusability among the services exposed.

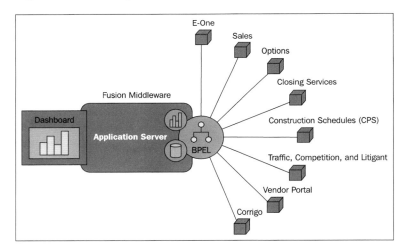

3. **Enable visibility**: By leveraging business events and sensors, Pardee Homes enhanced the visibility of the users into the integration across the enterprise and, more importantly, provided insight into integration errors. This enabled business users to monitor the health of the integration and take corrective action if a specific integration process failed. Also, users gained increased visibility into the automated purchase order and invoice approval process by using Oracle Human Workflow and its integration to the existing document management system. Reports provided to management identified task processing bottlenecks for quick resolution. SOA Governance provided visibility into all SOA artifacts and impact analysis of any changes.

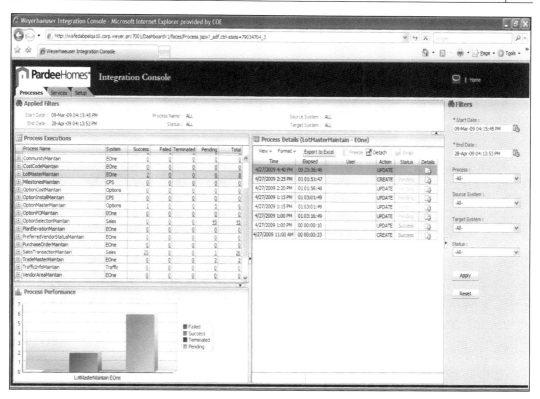

4. **Build Rich UI**: Two dashboards were developed using Oracle ADF. The first provided users with a real-time view to monitor transactions as they occur across the seven disparate systems that comprise the enterprise. This dashboard included features to resubmit or reinitiate failed transactions; users can also search for specific transactions using known business keys. This helps analyze the overall productivity and identify any bottlenecks in the flows, and also provides an easy way to search, monitor transactions, and recover failed transactions. The second dashboard provided users with a personalized view of their workflow tasks, bringing together documents from the FileNet content management system, purchase order and invoice data from the ERP application, and task information from Oracle Human workflow. This dashboard offered users a seamless UI experience in a rich Web 2.0 environment. Both dashboards leverage several of the reusable services described above.

The following table summarizes the Fusion development approach adopted by Pardee Homes.

Fusion development cycle	Pardee Homes approach
Model and analyze	Involved business and IT stakeholders to document and improve business processes using Oracle BPA Suite.
Create Service Layer	Leveraged Oracle AIA and Oracle SOA to define and build a layer of reusable services across their disparate applications.
Enable visibility	Business events used to initiate processes and sensors embedded in these processes fed to a dashboard to provide visibility into the integration errors. Oracle Human Workflow was used to enable visibility into approval workflow. Oracle SOA Governance provided visibility to all SOA artifacts.
Build Rich UI	Built dashboards using Oracle ADF to view integration errors, approval worklist, and to display documents that require approval.

This new solution enables the business to adjust quickly to market conditions when processes change. New sales are now immediately reflected in the customer service system. The completion of option construction is immediately reflected in the Vendor Portal, allowing vendors to bill quickly.

Summary

This chapter described and illustrated two approaches, Fusion Development (an application development process) and Oracle Enterprise Architecture (an architecture development framework and process). British Telecom's UniApp Framework and Pardee Homes' integration approach bear close resemblance to OEAF and Fusion development principles respectively. Fusion Development offers a new approach to assembling, rather than coding new business applications. Together with OEAF, Fusion Development offers an end-to-end approach to architect and build new composite applications that can be quickly developed, rapidly changed, and easily managed.

2

Process-driven SOA
Development

by Matjaz B. Juric and Harish Gaur

Business Process Management and SOA

One of the major benefits of a Service-Oriented Architecture is its ability to align IT with business processes. Business processes are important because they define the way business activities are performed. Business processes change as the company evolves and improves its operations. They also change in order to make the company more competitive.

Today, IT is an essential part of business operations. Companies are simply unable to do business without IT support. However, this places a high level of responsibility on IT. An important part of this responsibility is the ability of IT to react to changes in a quick and efficient manner. Ideally, IT must instantly respond to business process changes.

In most cases, however, IT is not flexible enough to adapt application architecture to the changes in business processes quickly. Software developers require time to modify application behavior. In the meantime, the company is stuck with old processes. In a highly competitive marketplace such delays are dangerous, and the threat is exacerbated by a reliance on traditional software development to make quick changes within an increasingly complex IT architecture.

The major problem with traditional approaches to software development is the huge semantic gap between IT and the process models. The traditional approach to software development has been focused on functionalities rather than on end-to-end support for business processes. It usually requires the definition of use cases, sequence diagrams, class diagrams, and other artifacts, which bring us to the actual code in a programming language such as Java, C#, C++, and so on. SOA reduces the semantic gap by introducing a development model that aligns the IT development cycle with the business process lifecycle. In SOA, business processes can be executed directly and integrated with existing applications through services.

To understand this better, let's look at the four phases of the SOA lifecycle:

- **Process modeling**: This is the phase in which process analysts work with process owners to analyze the business process and define the process model. They define the activity flow, information flow, roles, and business documents. They also define business policies and constraints, business rules, and performance measures. Performance measures are often called **Key Performance Indicators** (**KPIs**). Examples of KPIs include activity turnaround time, activity cost, and so on. Usually **Business Process Modeling Notation** (**BPMN**) is used in this phase.

- **Process implementation**: This is the phase in which developers work with process analysts to implement the business process, with the objective of providing end-to-end support for the process. In an SOA approach, the process implementation phase includes process implementation with the **Business Process Execution Language** (**BPEL**) and process decomposition to the services, implementation or reuse of services, and integration.

- **Process execution and control**: This is the actual execution phase, in which the process participants execute various activities of the process. In the end-to-end support for business processes, it is very important that IT drives the process and directs process participants to execute activities, and not vice versa, where the actual process drivers are employees. In SOA, processes execute on a process server. Process control is an important part of this phase, during which process supervisors or process managers control whether the process is executing optimally. If delays occur, exceptions arise, resources are unavailable, or other problems develop, process supervisors or managers can take corrective actions.

- **Process monitoring and optimization**: This is the phase in which process owners monitor the KPIs of the process using **Business Activity Monitoring** (**BAM**). Process analysts, process owners, process supervisors, and key users examine the process and analyze the KPIs while taking into account changing business conditions. They examine business issues and make optimizations to the business process.

The following figure shows how a process enters this cycle, and goes through the various stages:

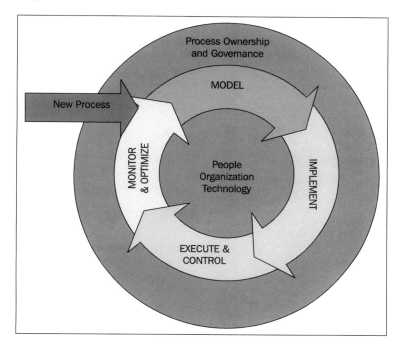

Once optimizations have been identified and selected, the process returns to the modeling phase, where optimizations are applied. Then the process is re-implemented and the whole lifecycle is repeated. This is referred to as an iterative-incremental lifecycle, because the process is improved at each stage.

Organizational aspects of SOA development

SOA development, as described in the previous section, differs considerably from traditional development. SOA development is process-centric and keeps the modeler and the developer focused on the business process and on end-to-end support for the process, thereby efficiently reducing the gap between business and IT.

The success of the SOA development cycle relies on correct process modeling. Only when processes are modeled in detail can we develop end-to-end support that will work. Exceptional process flows also have to be considered. This can be a difficult task, one that is beyond the scope of the IT department (particularly when viewed from the traditional perspective).

To make process-centric SOA projects successful, some organizational changes are required. Business users with a good understanding of the process must be motivated to actively participate in the process modeling. Their active participation must not be taken for granted, lest they find other work "more useful," particularly if they do not see the added value of process modeling. Therefore, a concise explanation as to why process modeling makes sense can be a very valuable time investment.

A good strategy is to gain top management support. It makes enormous sense to explain two key factors to top management—first, why a process centric approach and end-to-end support for processes makes sense, and second, why the IT department cannot successfully complete the task without the participation of business users. Usually top management will understand the situation rather quickly and will instruct business users to participate.

Obviously, the proposed process-centric development approach must become an ongoing activity. This will require the formalization of certain organizational structures. Otherwise, it will be necessary to seek approval for each and every project. We have already seen that the proposed approach outgrows the organizational limits of the IT department. Many organizations establish a BPM/SOA Competency Center, which includes business users and all the other profiles required for SOA development. This also includes the process analyst, process implementation, service development, and presentation layer groups, as well as SOA governance.

Perhaps the greatest responsibility of SOA development is to orchestrate the aforementioned groups so that they work towards a common goal. This is the responsibility of the project manager, who must work in close connection with the governance group. Only in this way can SOA development be successful, both in the short term (developing end-to-end applications for business processes), and in the long term (developing a flexible, agile IT architecture that is aligned with business needs).

Technology aspects of SOA development

SOA introduces technologies and languages that enable the SOA development approach. Particularly important is BPMN, which is used for business process modeling, and BPEL, which is used for business process execution.

BPMN is the key technology for process modeling. The process analyst group must have in-depth knowledge of BPMN and process modeling concepts. When modeling processes for SOA, they must be modeled in detail. Using SOA, we model business processes with the objective of implementing them in BPEL and executing them on the process server. Process models can be made executable only if all the relevant information is captured that is needed for the actual execution. We must identify individual activities that are atomic from the perspective of the execution. We must model exceptional scenarios too. Exceptional scenarios define how the process behaves when something goes wrong—and in the real world, business processes can and do go wrong. We must model how to react to exceptional situations and how to recover appropriately.

Next, we automate the process. This requires mapping of the BPMN process model into the executable representation in BPEL. This is the responsibility of the process implementation group. BPMN can be converted to BPEL almost automatically and vice versa, which guarantees that the process map is always in sync with the executable code. However, the executable BPEL process also has to be connected with the business services. Each process activity is connected with the corresponding business service. Business services are responsible for fulfilling the individual process activities.

SOA development is most efficient if you have a portfolio of business services that can be reused, and which includes lower-level and intermediate technical services. Business services can be developed from scratch, exposed from existing systems, or outsourced. This task is the responsibility of the service development group. In theory, it makes sense for the service development group to first develop all business services. Only then would the process implementation group start to compose those services into the process. However, in the real world this is often not the case, because you will probably not have the luxury of time to develop the services first and only then start the processes. And even if you do have enough time, it would be difficult to know which business services will be required by processes. Therefore, both groups usually work in parallel, which is a great challenge. It requires interaction between them and strict, concise supervision of the SOA governance group and the project manager; otherwise, the results of both groups (the process implementation group and the service development group) will be incompatible.

Once you have successfully implemented the process, it can be deployed on the process server. In addition to executing processes, a process server provides other valuable information, including a process audit trail, lists of successfully completed processes, and a list of terminated or failed processes. This information is helpful in controlling the process execution and in taking any necessary corrective measures. The services and processes communicate using the **Enterprise Service Bus** (**ESB**). The services and processes are registered in the UDDI-compliant service registry. Another part of the architecture is the rule engine, which serves as a central place for business rules. For processes with human tasks, user interaction is obviously important, and is connected to identity management.

The SOA platform also provides BAM. BAM helps to measure the key performance indicators of the process, and provides valuable data that can be used to optimize processes. The ultimate goal of each BAM user is to optimize process execution, to improve process efficiency, and to sense and react to important events.

BAM ensures that we start optimizing processes where it makes most sense. Traditionally, process optimization has been based on simulation results, or even worse, by guessing where bottlenecks might be. BAM, on the other hand, gives more reliable and accurate data, which leads to better decisions about where to start with optimizations. The following figure illustrates the SOA layers:

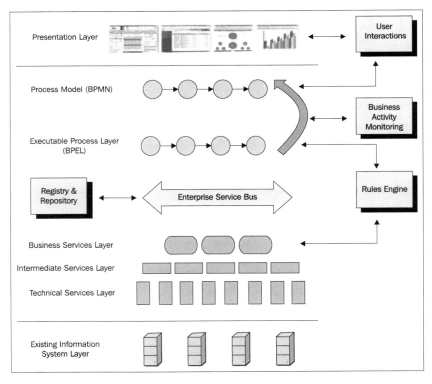

Case study: Process modeling

So far, we discussed the theory. Now let's take a look at a case study of an end-to-end procurement process from Elektro Slovenija, Slovenia's state-owned power distribution company. The procurement process was implemented using a full set of Oracle tools—Oracle Business Process Analysis PA Suite for the modeling, SOA Suite (BPEL Process Manager, ESB, Rules Author, WS Manager, Application Server) with JDeveloper, and Service Registry for the implementation, along with Oracle BAM for the business activity monitoring. The interrelationship is shown in the following figure:

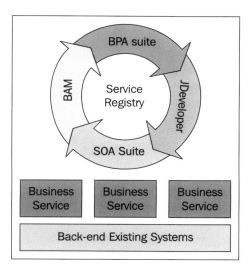

As a state-owned company, Elektro Slovenija must conform to strict regulations regarding procurement. The process starts with an order request form. First, a decision needs to be made as to whether the order will be collected with other similar orders for a joint purchase (for example, for office materials), or as an individual order. The order value influences the process as well. Orders smaller than €4,200 are the most simple and require that three offers are collected and that a purchase order is issued. For orders up to €12,000, a negotiation process takes place and a contract is issued. For larger orders, a special commission is created to carry out the ordering process, which differs depending on the type of order (product, service, or real estate). Several roles are involved in the process, including the order creator, the person responsible for the contract, the head of the procurement unit, and the commission for larger orders.

Modeling the process was the first challenge in the project. The company had already established an SOA Competency Center, and top management already had a good understanding of BPM and SOA. This simplified the situation, in that it was not very difficult to motivate business users to participate. In our experience, the group that models the process should include people in the following roles:

- Process owner, who will verify the process flow and make decisions about possible changes in the process.
- One or two process owner assistants with a solid understanding of the process. These individuals will do the actual modeling.
- Moderator, who will ask questions and lead the meeting.
- Process modeler, who is experienced in detailed SOA modeling.

The process in the BPA Suite has been modeled on six levels. It includes 24 sub-processes, and consists of 230 activities, of which more than 100 are human tasks. The process involves 25 different roles, implements more than 40 business rules, and defines seven key performance indicators. The following figure shows the BPA Suite application displaying the top-level process diagram:

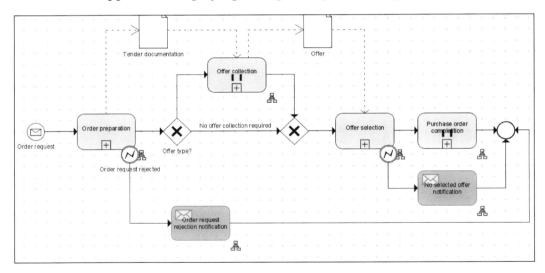

It is worth mentioning that the BPA Suite has good support for processes with human tasks (such as our example process). In addition, BPA Publisher can be used to share the process definition with other interested parties in order to foster collaboration.

Once the process has been designed, BPA Suite can check the model for semantic validity in order to indentify parts of the process that may have been incorrectly modeled, as illustrated in the following screenshot:

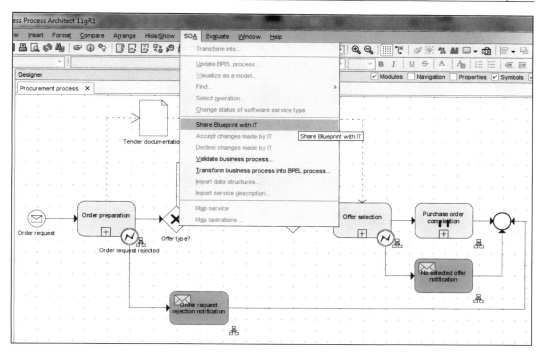

Case study: Process implementation

Three parallel development activities were started in order to develop the composite application for end-to-end support. They are:

- Development of the BPEL executable process
- Development of business services
- Development of the presentation layer—the user interface

In this case, the same team of two developers developed the BPEL executable process and the business services. One of those developers was also the process modeler. This simplified the organizational aspects and reduced the communication overhead.

The following subsections briefly describe the development of the BPEL executable process and the business services. However, the user interface is not SOA-specific, so it will not be discussed.

Development of BPEL executable process

The BPEL executable process can be developed manually, or it can be automatically translated from the BPMN model. We will use the latter approach, because with automatic translation we ensure consistency between the process model and the executable model. This approach also reduces effort, as it does not require developing BPEL from scratch. Finally, automatic translation can be applied in both directions, from BPMN to BPEL and vice versa, as we will see later. To enable seamless translation, several guidelines should be followed by the BPMN design (see the *Guidelines on BPMN to BPEL mapping* section covered later in this chapter). BPMN to BPEL transformation is very complex, and the same BPMN construct can be mapped to BPEL in different ways.

If you follow the guidelines, the transformation from BPMN to BPEL (from BPA Suite to JDeveloper blueprint) is straightforward. While the technology is relatively new, it works well enough for production use on complex processes, such as this procurement process. Our experience with the transformation has been mostly positive. The following screenshot shows the JDeveloper BPEL Blueprint perspective.

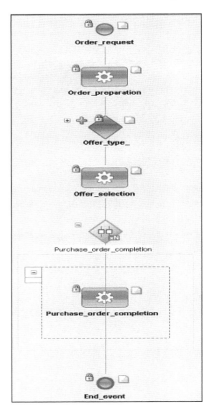

The BPEL code has to be amended in JDeveloper. The most important task here is to connect the BPEL process with the actual business services. Please note that the WSDL interfaces of the business services can be used in the BPA Suite already. This means that we do not have to wait until the development phase (in JDeveloper, where it is obvious that we will use WSDL interfaces). This way we can make the process model conformant with business service interfaces in the design phase, which can simplify BPEL development. Such an approach, however, requires some additional skills from the process modelers.

In addition to connecting BPEL with services, other important activities of this phase include development of ESB mediations, registering services in the Service Registry, entering business rules into the Rules Author, deploying the process, and developing the BAM dashboard (which we will talk about later).

Development of business services

The procurement process had to be integrated with several existing applications, particularly the business information system applications, including accounting, general ledger, and inventory. Not all applications had service interfaces; therefore, some new interfaces had to be developed and business logic exposed through services. When exposing existing applications as services, it is crucial to have support from the original developers. Otherwise, service developers will waste a lot of time struggling through legacy code. In this case, existing applications have been Oracle Forms applications. The procurement process also deals with quite a few documents, including the order request, tender documentation, offers, a contract, purchase order, and several others. To manage electronic versions of the documents, an e-document content management system has been used. Although Oracle Universal Content Management would be the obvious choice, the company already had another content management system deployed, which had service interfaces. This made the task of integrating it quite straightforward. When developing business services, it is important to follow SOA patterns and, in particular, the loose-coupling principle. It is also important to develop reusable business services.

BPMN to BPEL Round-tripping

An important part of SOA development, particularly in real-world projects, is the ability to round-trip changes between the BPMN model in BPA Suite and BPEL in the JDeveloper blueprint representation. There are two important aspects of round-tripping:

- How changes in the BPMN model can be propagated to BPEL without losing implementation changes already done in BPEL
- How changes done in BPEL can be propagated back to the BPMN model, to keep them both in sync

We have been pleasantly surprised by the maturity of Oracle tools. In both scenarios, the round-tripping experience has been positive:

- When updating the BPA process model, we have been able to propagate changes to the JDeveloper blueprint without losing previous implementation changes to the BPEL.

- When updating the BPEL in JDeveloper, we have been able to propagate the changes back to the BPA model, where the business people had the choice to accept or decline the changes. The following screenshots illustrate an example where a Save Order request activity has been added in BPEL (in JDeveloper) and the change has been propagated to the BPMN model in BPA Suite.

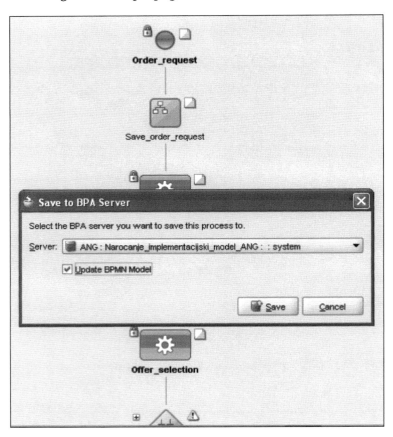

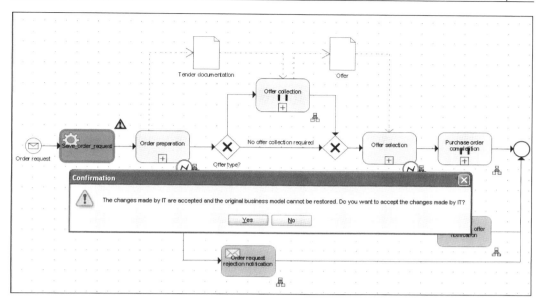

Round-tripping is very important for real-world development, as it is the key to iterative SOA development, which guarantees short development cycles and easy modifications to existing composite applications. Round-tripping also keeps the model (BPMN) and the executable code (BPEL) in sync. Our experience with Oracle tools revealed only very minor problems, such as fault handlers that did not synchronize properly between BPA and JDeveloper. In our opinion, the approach taken by Oracle, where the modeling and implementation tools are separate, is better than the approach that uses the same tool for both.

Guidelines on BPMN to BPEL mapping

Let's take another look at the BPMN to BPEL mapping. We learned that in BPA Suite not all BPMN constructs map equally well to BPEL. Therefore, a process modeler must be aware of the specifics related to the BPMN to BPEL mapping in order to get the most efficient model.

The basic rules for mapping are:

- All BPMN activities are mapped to BPEL scopes
- Start events are mapped to receive or pick activities, depending on the type of trigger
- End events are mapped to reply, invoke, throw, or other activities, depending on the type
- Gateways are transformed to different BPEL activities, such as pick, switch, or flow

- Business data is mapped to variables
- Subprocesses are mapped to invoke activities
- Each BPMN subprocess becomes a separate BPEL process

Particular care must be exercised when dealing with the cycles. BPMN supports arbitrary cycles, but BPEL does not. Therefore, we must convert all cycles to while loops (structured cycles). This, however, can change the process model considerably, at least from the visual perspective (the process behavior is unchanged if the appropriate conversion is performed). As a result, business people might have trouble understanding the converted model. The lack of support for arbitrary cycles can also be a problem if the process has many interleaved human tasks.

To avoid structured cycles in simpler scenarios, we can do some refactoring for decisions with multiple outputs. Such decisions should be decomposed into multiple decisions. For example, the following scenario does not map appropriately to BPEL:

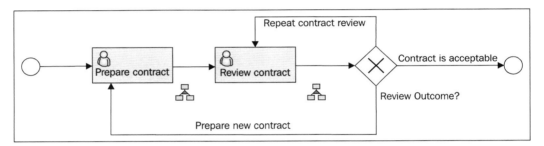

Therefore, we should decompose the decision into two decisions as follows:

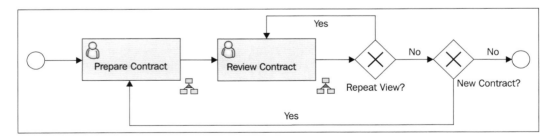

The activities in cycles, which repeat, are duplicated in the generated BPEL. This can be avoided by grouping the repeating activities and modeling them as subprocesses. Then, only the invoke activity for calling the subprocess will be repeated in the generated BPEL.

Exercise caution with the end events, which do not actually end the BPEL process, as you might expect. In BPMN decisions we can influence how the generated BPEL switch will be generated. If we do not define the default flow for a condition, an otherwise is generated within the BPEL switch activity. This can be useful, particularly for human tasks where the BPEL process should check for a variety of possible human task outcomes.

Process execution

After successful development, the composite application is deployed to the process server. Oracle SOA Suite and BPEL Process Manager in particular provide adequate tools to control and manage the process execution. Particularly, the added fault policies in 10.1.3.4 are very useful in production use, as they allow system administrator intervention if a fault occurs in the process. The procurement process is a long-running process that includes several human tasks. So the process must not be terminated if a fault occurs. Fault policies support this and allow a separation of the system fault handling from the process implementation. WS Manager is a useful tool in the process execution phase. It simplifies supervision of the process and services, and allows usage monitoring and even SLA compliance control.

Processes that include human tasks also require an identity management system, with all the roles and users that participate in the process. In our case, we used Active Directory, which can be integrated with the SOA Suite. Alternatively, we could have used Oracle Identity Management.

Process monitoring using BAM and optimizations

Legislative changes in the past made several modifications necessary to the procurement process. In addition, the company's efforts to increase efficiency, which placed a high priority on the ability to systematically identify process bottlenecks, further increased the need for process modification.

To support this, we have implemented BAM support. This includes the definition of sensors to monitor the process execution and the development of a BAM dashboard. The following screenshot shows an example dashboard developed for the process:

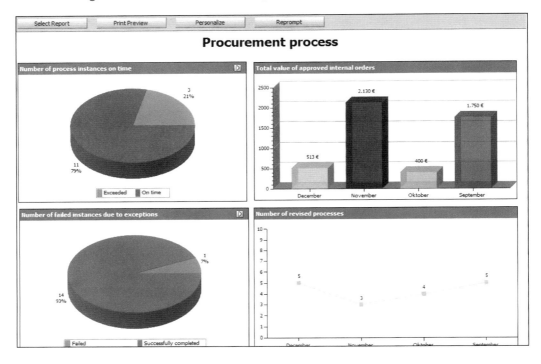

BAM has proved particularly important for process owners, who are able to monitor the process execution in real time. In our experience, developing a BAM dashboard is quite simple, at least for monitoring simple KPIs.

The final challenge was to import the BAM data back into the BPA modeling tool. This can be done using custom JavaScript, but it's quite time consuming. Future versions of BPA Suite will improve on this and make things easier.

BAM data is a useful starting point for process optimizations. So far, the procurement process is only in its first iteration, and has not yet been optimized. However, BAM data has already been used to identify possible optimization points. Even in its first iteration, the procurement process has demonstrated several benefits—the workload on the employees is reduced by 25% to 35%, as some process activities have been automated, and the visibility of the process is considerably improved. It is possible to track the execution of the process instances and to figure out which activity is occurring within a selected process instance. This reduces gap times, which leads to faster execution. In future iterations, more process steps will be automated, which will result in even higher benefits.

Summary

As a real-world example, the case study has proved the most important benefits of a process-centric SOA approach—better alignment between business and IT, faster development cycles, fewer errors, and most important, much faster development cycles, which guarantee considerable reduction in the time required to fulfill business requirements.

Related to better alignment between business and IT, the following important benefits of process-centric development also emerged:

- Better understanding of business requirements
- End-to-end business process support
- Process monitoring and execution control, which provides valuable business performance indicators

These benefits would have been very difficult to achieve without an SOA approach.

We also learned that the process-centric approach to SOA development is both a technical and an organizational challenge. It requires the setting up of competent groups for process modeling, process implementation, service development, and the development of the user interface. It also requires the setting up of necessary supervision, through SOA governance and project management. For smaller projects, the same small development group can take over several roles. Finally, SOA development requires new skills to be successful.

The benefits of the complete SOA process lifecycle, spanning modeling, implementation, execution, monitoring, and optimization, are numerous and well worth the necessary investment in the required knowledge and products. We believe that covering the full process lifecycle shows the real value of SOA, which will be even more obvious when changes, modifications, and optimizations are made to the process.

The main message of this case study is that it is possible to develop a complete end-to-end process for a complex real-world process. The process-centric approach to SOA development with full lifecycle support encompasses enormous opportunities for companies to improve and optimize not only their IT support but also their operational efficiency through process automation.

Further Reading:

- Matjaz Juric, Kapil Pant, Business Process Driven SOA using BPMN and BPEL, Packt Publishing, August 2008 (`https://www.packtpub.com/business-process-driven-SOA-using-BPMN-and-BPEL/book`)

- Matjaz Juric, Poornachandra Sarang, Benny Mathew, Business Process Execution Language for Web Services 2nd Edition, Packt Publishing, January 2006 (`https://www.packtpub.com/bpel2e/book`)

- Matjaz B. Juric, Marcel Krizevnik, WS-BPEL 2.0 for SOA Composite Applications with Oracle SOA Suite 11*g*, Packt Publishing, September 2010 (`https://www.packtpub.com/ws-bpel-2-0-for-soa-with-oracle-soa-suite-11g/book`)

3

Code-free Application Extensions and Integrations

by Sandeep Banerjie, Srikant Subramaniam, and Nikhilesh Chitnis

In today's fast-paced business environment, customer preferences, business models, enabling technologies, and regulations change quickly. Organizations must anticipate change, even embrace it, if they are to improve operational excellence, increase customer focus, expand profitable relationships, and remain leaders in their industries.

For many businesses, however, IT lacks the capacity to support fast, fluid business change. Invasive application extensions and integrations are among the factors that contribute to this problem.

Very often, attempts are made to close business and IT gaps through the customization and integration of existing ERP, CRM, SCM, and similar applications. But a shotgun approach to implementing these modifications, with little regard for standards and enterprise architecture principles, is likely to exacerbate the problem. Traditional implementation practices for such modifications are typically invasive in nature and introduce risk into projects, affect time-to-market and ease of use, and ultimately increase the costs of running and maintaining the applications.

So, if archaic integration techniques make up nearly 20% of an application's initial implementation costs, and invasive customizations result in nearly 50% of total upgrade costs, adopting innovative solutions to change the economics of integration becomes an imperative rather than a choice.

We are seeing a rapid growth in the adoption of **Service-Oriented Architecture (SOA)**, **Business Process Management (BPM)**, **Business Intelligence (BI)**, Web 2.0, and the more recent phenomenon of Cloud Computing in order to address many of these challenges. In a nutshell, we are evolving to the next generation of IT capabilities and services.

In this chapter, using a real-life customer example, we will illustrate how you can use SOA, BPM, Web 2.0, and BI to extend and integrate Oracle applications without writing a single line of code. The approach makes these modifications simple, quick to implement, and easy to maintain/upgrade. It offers an innovative and practical solution to radically change the economics of running your Oracle applications.

Customer scenario: Travel and expense management

A global payments technology company with 5000+ employees wants to automate its highly manual and time- and cost-intensive travel authorization process.

The automation will allow employees to submit travel authorization requests online and enable managers to analyze, review, and approve (or reject) requests online. This automation will improve the company's travel and expense management process and reduce operational costs.

The solution will involve extending their backend travel and expense reimbursement system, which does not support this specific requirement out-of-the-box.

IT has three choices to deliver this solution:

- Native customization of backend travel and expense reimbursement system
- Bolt-on "niche" application for travel authorization
- Code-free extension and integration of a backend travel and expense reimbursement system

Native customization of backend travel and expense reimbursement system

It is most common among packaged application users to first try to fit functionality enhancements or set new requirements directly within the application.

In this case, Oracle E-Business Suite (iExpense) is the travel expense reimbursement system. To deliver this capability, Oracle E-Business Suite has to be customized (extended) and integrated. This customization would involve developing custom **Oracle Application** (**OA**) framework pages through which a user can submit authorization requests. Custom look-up types will have to be created for **Oracle Approvals Management** (**AME**) and for workflow processes to run. The workflow packages and AME rules will have to be integrated. Existing iExpense pages (such as an approver's page) will have to be modified to accommodate the additional functionality, including adding and hiding fields, menus, functions, messages, buttons, and so on. Custom tables will have to be built, including create, update, delete, insert, and rollback functions. New reports will have to be generated.

The estimated effort to build the solution using this method is approximately 70 person-days.

Bolt-on niche application for travel authorization

Many times, packaged application users adopt the bolt-on strategy to deliver missing functionality and avoid customization within the backend application. This typically involves integrating a **Commercial off-the-shelf** (**COTS**) niche solution or a custom application with different systems. This approach can provide greater feature-function fit with lower configuration effort, but in most cases it increases the overall cost of the solution, especially when you take into consideration the software support fees and staff costs to run and maintain the solution.

In the case of the travel authorization scenario, the solution (either COTS or custom) would be tailored specifically for E-Business Suite. It would be a siloed implementation with its own solution lifecycle, and would not serve as the single standardized platform for application extensions and customizations.

The estimated effort to build the solution using this method is approximately 20 person-days.

Code-free extension and integration of a backend travel and expense reimbursement system

This method leverages an integrated SOA, BPM, Web 2.0, and BI applications platform to provide a code-free assembly approach to application extensions and integrations. The solution includes a rich and intelligent Web 2.0 user interface for submitting and approving travel authorization requests. It seamlessly integrates with the Oracle E-Business Suite-iExpense module using SOA. BPM automates the different travel authorization profiles requiring myriad rules, workflows, and integrations. BI applications deliver process intelligence and historical analysis, allowing employees and managers to make more informed decisions.

The estimated effort to build the solution using this method is approximately 10 person-days.

A summary of the key characteristics of the three solution deployment choices and their relative impact on time, cost, ease of use, and investment protection are seen in the following tables.

The key characteristics of the solution deployment choices are:

Choices 1 and 2	Choice 3
Build for permanence	Build for change
Tightly coupled to backend application	Loosely coupled as a composite application on top of backend application
Application function-driven	Business process-driven
Collaboration is hard	Collaboration is ingrained
Process intelligence is limited	Process intelligence is ingrained
Homogenous vertical integration	Heterogeneous horizontal integration

The relative impact of the solution deployment choices is:

Choices	Time	Cost	Ease of Use	Investment Protection
Native Customization	High	Medium	Low	Medium
Bolt-on Niche Application	Low	High	High	Low
Code-free Extensions and Integrations	Low	Low	High	High

These tables suggest that the integrated platform approach offers the best overall solution, one that is designed for the way people work, and built to be changed as needed. This solution enables new levels of agility, creates compelling user experiences, generates additional productivity, and delivers competitive advantage.

The integrated platform approach requires about 85 percent less effort to build the solution when compared to traditional approaches like native customization and integration of backend applications. This approach can also reduce upgrade costs by about 40 percent. You can learn more about this in the Oracle white paper *Application Upgrades and Service Oriented Architecture* (`http://www.oracle.com/technologies/soa/docs/soa-application-upgrades.pdf`).

Let us now discuss the architectural concepts and components that make up the integrated platform for delivering code-free application extensions and integrations.

Programming code-free application extensions and integrations—the platform

The travel authorization solution uses Oracle Fusion Middleware as the integrated platform for code-free extensions and integrations. The different components of the solution are seen in the following figure. SOA is at the core of this integrated platform. It introduces a layered architecture, designed to eliminate code, minimize IT maintenance costs, and accelerate speed of change across the entire IT landscape composed of multiple business applications.

Each component in the following figure plays an important role and contributes to the overall time, cost, ease of use, and investment protection of the solution, as outlined in the earlier table showing the relative impact of solution deployment choices.

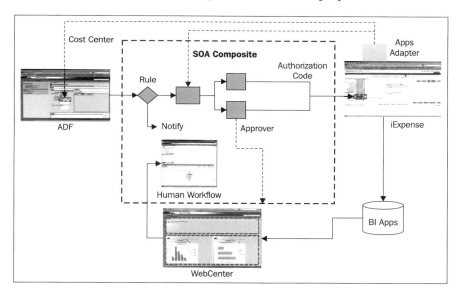

We will discuss each of the following components in detail:

- Oracle Internet Expenses
- Application Development Framework (ADF)
- SOA Composite
- WebCenter

E-Business Suite-iExpense

E-Business Suite-iExpense is a backend travel and expense management application. It enables the entry and submission of expense reports using a standard web browser or a web-enabled mobile device. Oracle Workflow automatically routes expense reports for approval and enforces reimbursement policies. Oracle iExpense integrates with Oracle Payables to provide for the quick processing of expense reports for payment.

The Oracle E-Business Suite Adapter provides connectivity by exposing the E-Business Suite's interfaces as Web Services. These Web Services can, in turn, be composed into an SOA-based integration solution between business processes across enterprise applications, using Oracle Fusion Middleware. The Adapter supports several integration technologies, including PL/SQL APIs (as used in this scenario), Business Events, Open Interface Tables, Concurrent Programs, XML Messages, e-Commerce Gateway Interface, and Interface Views.

Application Development Framework (ADF)

Application Development Framework is the 4GL development tool used to expose E-Business Suite Web Services on a web page. It is shipped with **Oracle JDeveloper**. With ADF, SOA Composite, and E-Business Suite Adapter, Web Services can be exposed without a single line of code due to the power of its data controls, as well as JDeveloper's visual page layouts and page flows.

For the travel authorization solution, the Travel Authorization portlet is built using ADF. All user interactions are implemented using ADF task flows. The task flows provide a modular approach for defining control flow in an application. Instead of representing an application as a single large development component (for example, a **Java Server Faces** (**JSF**) page flow), you can break it up into a collection of reusable task flows, each of which contains a portion of the application's navigational graph. The nodes in the task flows are activities. An activity node represents a simple logical operation such as displaying a page, executing application logic, or calling another task flow. The application can therefore be broken up into a series of individual task flows that call one another. These task flows containing common functionality can be packaged into a library that can be shared between different developers, across different teams, and even across departments within an organization. This kind of modularity facilitates reuse, thereby significantly reducing the time and effort needed to put up and maintain applications.

For more information on building end-to-end enterprise-class (Java EE) web applications using Oracle ADF, refer to *Oracle Application Development Framework: Tutorial for Forms/4GL Developers* (`http://www.oracle.com/technology/obe/ADFBC_tutorial_1013/10131/index.htm`).

SOA Composite

SOA Composite helps to integrate E-Business Suite Web Services with other systems and processes. This is done using **Business Process Execution Language** (**BPEL**), the standard for orchestrating Web Services and **Enterprise Service Bus** (**ESB**) for queuing and messaging purposes. It is shipped with **Oracle SOA Suite**. BPEL allows you to create processes that orchestrate Web Services. The end result is end-to-end processes spanning E-Business Suite and other applications, as well as data integrations from (and to) E-Business Suite that can leverage process logic for error handling and exception management.

Approval flows in the travel authorization solution (including human workflow and rules) are automated by SOA Composite. The tight integration of SOA Suite and E-Business Suite provides the capability to dynamically extract the approval hierarchy for the human workflow. During run time, automated workflows help reduce errors, eliminate repetitive entries, and enforce approval procedures. During design time, Oracle BPEL Process Manager makes it possible to visually design processes that orchestrate Web Services exposed from E-Business Suite as well as other applications.

For more information on service enabling E-Business Suite with Oracle BPEL Process Manager and Enterprise Services Bus, see:

- **BPEL**: Service Oracle Enable E-Business Suite with Oracle SOA Suite BPEL Process Manager (`http://www.oracle.com/technology/tech/fmw4apps/ebs/obe/OOW08-EBS-BPEL.pdf`)

- **ESB**: Propagating eBusiness Suite Business Events with Enterprise Service Bus (`http://www.oracle.com/technology/obe/fusion_middleware/fusion/soa/ebuz_esb/ebusiness_events_esb.htm`)

WebCenter

WebCenter delivers role-based content to business users, allowing users to tailor their work environments to meet specific needs, and supports the creation of a collaborative environment for project teams to manage their projects and content without requiring IT assistance. It is shipped with **Oracle WebCenter Spaces**. WebCenter also includes the ability to embed **Oracle Universal Content Management** stores to manage documents.

The travel authorization solution makes use of **WebCenter Spaces** to allow business users to customize their workspace and content. Different types of content are delivered based on user role:

- Employee:
  - Custom Travel Authorization portlet

- Travel Auditor
  - Compliance documents repository
  - Task worklist

- Management
  - Task worklist
  - **Oracle Business Intelligence Applications (BI Apps)** analytic dashboards

The drag-and-drop features in WebCenter Spaces and the integration with BI dashboard portlets expedite overall web page assembly and content distribution.

For more information on integrating E-Business Suite in a WebCenter application, refer to *Integrating Oracle E-Business Suite in a WebCenter Application* (`http://www.oracle.com/technology/obe/fusion_middleware/fusion/adf_wc/10_133_ebs_webcenter/ebs_webcenter.htm`).

BI Apps deliver a packaged analytics solution that eliminates the need to develop data warehouse design, extract Transform Load logic from the sources, and provide best practice dashboards.

Within the travel authorization solution, BI Apps provide pre-built ETL routines which capture data at the end of each day from E-Business Suite and then upload that data to the BI Apps data store. This data is then delivered via WebCenter Spaces to business users, who can then make informed decisions.

The following figure illustrates the overall travel authorization workflow, involving system- and human-centric processes:

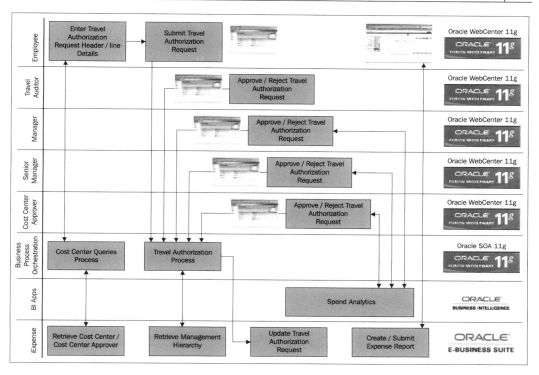

1. Employees sign onto the Travel Authorization Portal with WebCenter to raise travel related requests. The portal page has:

   ° A list of existing travel authorization requests submitted by the employee with their respective status

   ° A link to submit a new travel authorization request

   ° A group calendar of people traveling to various events across the country

   ° My Buddy List

   ° Travel alerts using RSS feeds

2. Clicking on the **Submit new travel request** presents a data entry form to submit a travel authorization request with the following information:

   ° First Name

   ° Last Name

   ° Travel Date

- ° Destination
- ° Event (populated from a central data store)
- ° Cost center (information retrieved from E-Business Suite)
- ° Amount
- ° Subcategory (includes options like Companion travel with downgrade, Companion travel without downgrade, Decline use of preferred hotels, Decline lowest fare)
- ° Weather information for the specified city and date using ADF task flows

3. The travel request is then routed through a workflow using BPEL to different approvers depending on the approval amount. It also appears in the employee's portal page as a list of submitted requests.

4. The request is first routed to the travel auditor who is able to see the list of pending travel requests in his WebCenter portal page. This information is rendered from the BPEL `worklist` application.

5. If the approval amount is greater than US$1,000, a notification is sent in parallel to the employee's manager using Business Rules and BPEL.

6. Upon approval by the travel auditor, using BPEL the travel request is routed in parallel to:
   - ° Cost center approver (information is retrieved from E-Business Suite)
   - ° Manager and Senior Manager of the employee (hierarchy is retrieved from E-Business Suite)

7. The cost center approver, Manager, and Senior Manager access the travel request from their respective WebCenter portal pages. Based on spend analytics such as employee T&E history, departmental budgets versus actual, and so on delivered as dashboards within the portal page by BI Applications, approvers make an informed decision to approve/reject the travel request.

8. Once approved by all stakeholders, the travel request information is updated in E-Business Suite-iExpense and an e-mail notification is sent to the travel desk. If rejected by any approver, the travel request is closed and notification is sent to the employee.

9. For approved travel requests, upon completion of travel, employees log in to E-Business Suite-iExpense to submit their expense report and associate the expense line items with the travel authorization request previously updated in E-Business Suite.

An MVC approach to creating a composite UI with ADF, SOA, and JDeveloper

SOA Composite, along with the E-Business Suite Adapter, is used to expose the cost center information from E-Business Suite as the Web Service `retrieveCostCenter`. A set of data controls within Oracle ADF integrates the `retrieveCostCenter` Web Service and delivers the data to the travel authorization application.

Oracle ADF's 4GL programming and the pre-built connectivity between the components allows for these data controls to be built without a single line of code. Oracle ADF task flows, created using Oracle JDeveloper, lay out the navigational aspects of the custom travel authorization application, as shown in the following screenshot:

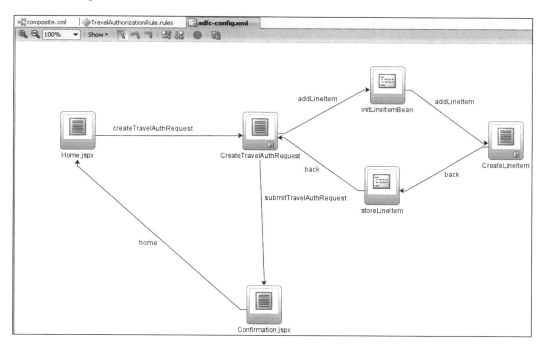

Clicking on a **View object** in the page flow allows you to design a specific view of the travel authorization application, as seen in the following screenshot. These views or pages are designed using ADF's drag-and-drop features.

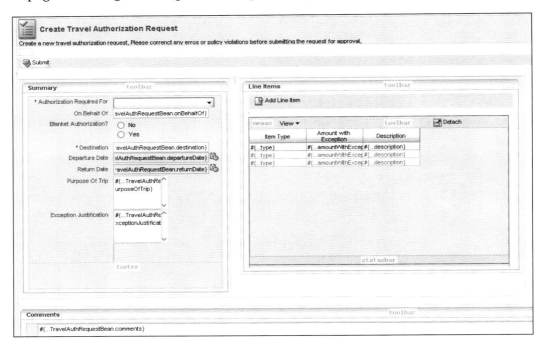

Oracle JDeveloper uses the **WSDL (Web Services Description Language)** of the deployed service (in this case `retrieveCostCenter`) to introspect and auto-generate the necessary bindings for invocation. The data control is auto-generated and displayed in a palette in Oracle JDeveloper, as shown in the next screenshot. This data control is then used to bind the retrieved cost center to a display component on the page and bind it to other view components, buttons, and so on.

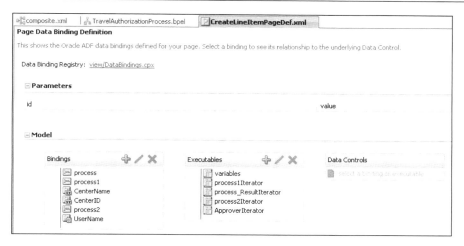

Integrating with E-Business Suite using Oracle SOA and Oracle application adapter

The travel authorization solution uses the SOA Composite to dynamically retrieve the list of approvers from E-Business Suite during runtime. This list is then used to drive the workflow for the request.

A BPEL process retrieves the organization hierarchy from the E-Business Suite instance. The integration is established with the Oracle Applications adapter. In this case, a custom PL/SQL API is created in E-Business Suite using a PL/SQL interface to retrieve or update data, as shown next:

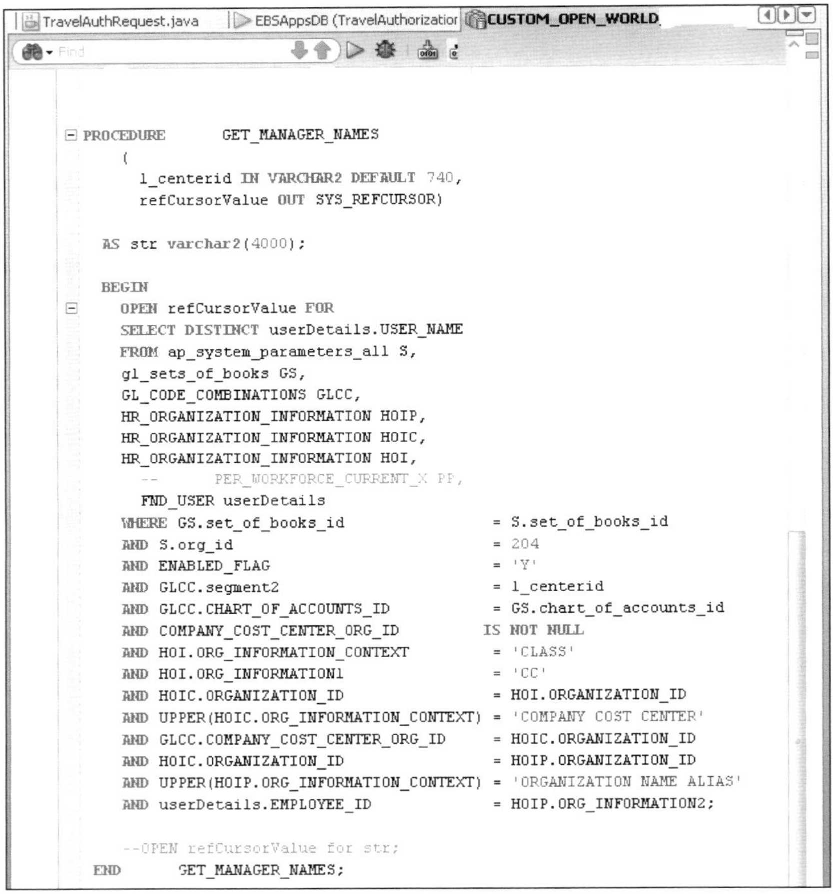

```
 TravelAuthRequest.java     EBSAppsDB (TravelAuthorizatior  CUSTOM_OPEN_WORLD
  - Find                           ▶

  ⊟ PROCEDURE        GET_MANAGER_NAMES
         (
             l_centerid IN VARCHAR2 DEFAULT 740,
             refCursorValue OUT SYS_REFCURSOR)

      AS str varchar2(4000);

      BEGIN
  ⊟      OPEN refCursorValue FOR
         SELECT DISTINCT userDetails.USER_NAME
         FROM ap_system_parameters_all S,
         gl_sets_of_books GS,
         GL_CODE_COMBINATIONS GLCC,
         HR_ORGANIZATION_INFORMATION HOIP,
         HR_ORGANIZATION_INFORMATION HOIC,
         HR_ORGANIZATION_INFORMATION HOI,
             --      PER_WORKFORCE_CURRENT_X PP,
           FND_USER userDetails
         WHERE GS.set_of_books_id              = S.set_of_books_id
         AND S.org_id                          = 204
         AND ENABLED_FLAG                      = 'Y'
         AND GLCC.segment2                     = l_centerid
         AND GLCC.CHART_OF_ACCOUNTS_ID         = GS.chart_of_accounts_id
         AND COMPANY_COST_CENTER_ORG_ID        IS NOT NULL
         AND HOI.ORG_INFORMATION_CONTEXT       = 'CLASS'
         AND HOI.ORG_INFORMATION1              = 'CC'
         AND HOIC.ORGANIZATION_ID              = HOI.ORGANIZATION_ID
         AND UPPER(HOIC.ORG_INFORMATION_CONTEXT) = 'COMPANY COST CENTER'
         AND GLCC.COMPANY_COST_CENTER_ORG_ID   = HOIC.ORGANIZATION_ID
         AND HOIC.ORGANIZATION_ID              = HOIP.ORGANIZATION_ID
         AND UPPER(HOIP.ORG_INFORMATION_CONTEXT) = 'ORGANIZATION NAME ALIAS'
         AND userDetails.EMPLOYEE_ID           = HOIP.ORG_INFORMATION2;

         --OPEN refCursorValue for str;
      END        GET_MANAGER_NAMES;
```

The Oracle Applications adapter provides a visual interface to browse and access APIs (custom and public) from E-Business Suite. The following screenshot illustrates how the OA adapter also provides connectivity to these APIs as Web Services:

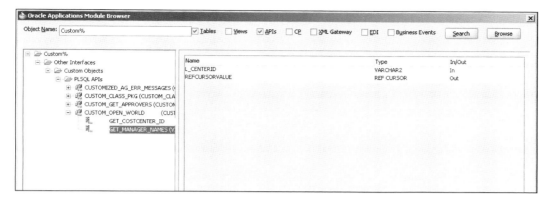

Once the adapter is configured, it is consumed in the BPEL process using an Invoke activity.

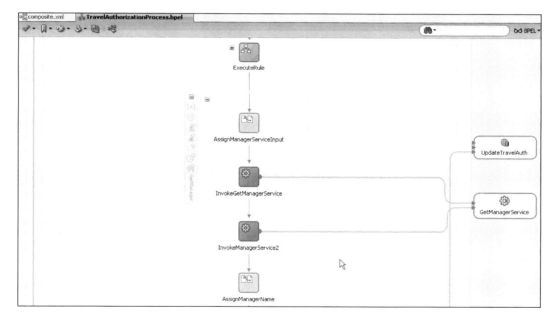

At this point the data (list of approvers) from E-Business Suite is retrieved based on the following variables:

1. `FirstLevelManager`
2. `SecondLevelManager`

The list is exposed as a Web Service and is readily consumed by the main BPEL process and assigned internally to human tasks to drive the workflow.

Building business logic using Oracle SOA and Oracle Business Rules

The travel authorization solution uses a business rule to determine if a travel authorization request requires additional approval. These business rules are implemented via **Oracle Business Rules** (**OBR**), a component of Oracle SOA Suite. OBR integrates with applications via rules and decision tables. This integration is achieved via the use of Oracle JDeveloper as the single tool for modeling business terms, rules, and processes—without writing a single line of code. The OBR component is wired to the overall business process using the SOA Composite Editor, as shown in the following screenshot:

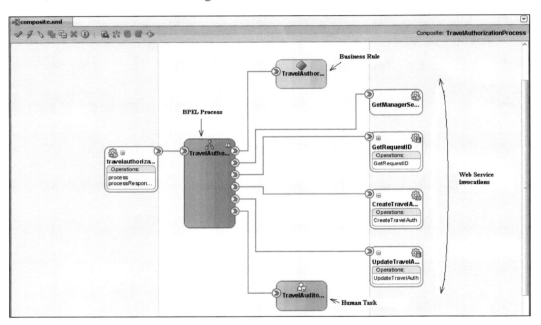

Modeling is often an iterative activity. For example, a new rule might require a new business term or it might specify an outcome that requires a change to the business process. In this situation integrated tools can make business analysts more productive. While the **Oracle Business Rules Designer** extension to JDeveloper enables the design-time creation of business rules, the SOA Composer allows users to view, edit, and commit changes to business rules at runtime via a user-friendly web interface, without the need to redeploy the entire application.

A business rule is comprised of **IF** and **THEN** parts. The IF part tests one or more business terms. Once this test is passed, one or more actions are performed in the THEN part. For instance, the travel authorization solution has a rule that requires additional approval if the amount exceeds US$1,000. OBR Designer can be used to model this rule, as shown in the following screenshot:

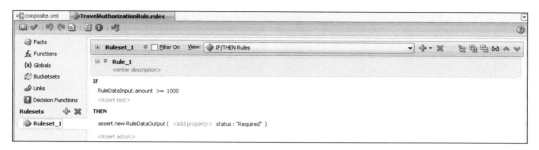

Building the BI dashboard with Oracle BI Application Spend Analytics

Oracle BI Applications include prebuilt **ETL** (**Extract, Transform, and Load**) adapters and business logic to tap into a multitude of common operations applications and data sources, including E-Business Suite, Siebel CRM, PeopleSoft, JD Edwards, call center operational information such as **IVR** (**Interactive Voice Response**) and **CTI** (**Computer Telephony Integration**) data, web logs, and a host of other systems. The Repository content pre-packaged with Oracle BI Applications consists of the source system mappings from these different data sources.

With the help of the repository, we can graphically select the source, in this case, E-Business Suite. Then, historical spend information for the employee is retrieved from E-Business Suite and loaded in BI Data Warehouse with the pre-built ETL. The mapping from the source is extracted to a temporary staging for relevant changes, as shown in the following screenshots:

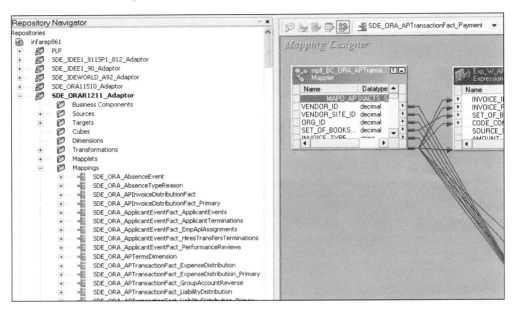

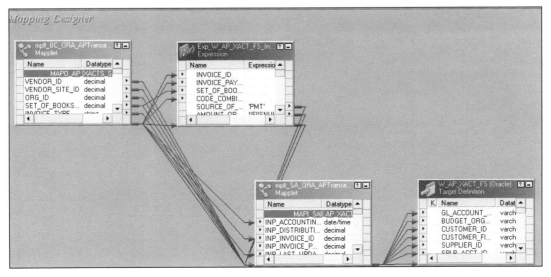

Based on this extracted data, BI delivers the spend analytics as dashboards, which are looked over by travel approvers for more informed decision-making.

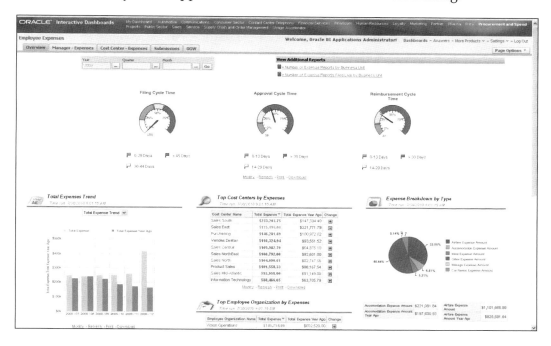

Beyond the travel authorization solution—an approach for other applications

The strategies and solutions presented in this article for extending and integrating applications with the Oracle Fusion Middleware platform can be applied to other Oracle applications, including Siebel, PeopleSoft, JD Edwards, and Agile, as well as to non-Oracle applications. The Oracle Fusion Middleware Best Practice Centers offer a broad selection of step-by-step guides and tutorials that illustrate how to service-enable Oracle applications and build integrations, business processes, and composite applications without writing code.

Summary

The next generation of IT principles, SOA, BPM, Web 2.0, and BI, will make business applications work the way business users perform tasks, with inherent intelligence, collaboration, and information access, along with components that can be reused, shared, and aggregated. The resulting dynamic applications, highly interactive and collaborative by design, and capable of being quickly assembled with data sources from inside and outside the business, will be adaptable in real time to suit situational changes.

Invasive customizations and extensions of backend applications are an impediment to building dynamic business applications. As illustrated in this chapter, Oracle Fusion Middleware offers an open and integrated platform for Applications Unlimited customers to simplify application extensions and integrations, improve process visibility, and resolve process quality gaps. Oracle's Fusion Platform changes the economics of running Oracle applications, both for new implementations and for upgrades. With the Oracle Fusion Middleware Platform, Applications Unlimited customers can immediately leverage code-free extensions and integrations and other capabilities without the need for technical upgrades to Oracle Fusion Applications.

4

Data Tier Caching for SOA Performance

by Kiran Dattani, Milind Pandit, and Markus Zirn

Service-Oriented Architecture (SOA) is changing the application development and integration game. Web Service standards make it possible to reuse existing business logic much more easily, independent of the way that specific technology in the business logic is implemented. BPEL and other orchestration standards make it easy to string together such services via composite process flows. Hence, SOA provides ways to *access* information as well as *combine* information more easily.

This leads to significant benefits, notably improved agility, and enhanced productivity thanks to better interoperability across existing monolithic applications. At the same time, SOA also raises the bar for IT because business users have higher expectations. Business users, now familiar with using consumer Internet applications and mash-ups from Google, Yahoo, and other companies demand similar capabilities from their enterprise systems. SOA helps to implement such mash-ups.

The downside to this positive development is performance. Performance and scalability issues have grown to be one of the topmost concerns when building an SOA application. This concern is not surprising. The results of an SOA composite application are surfaced in a user interface and therefore bound by an acceptable response time. Users typically consider any results beyond five seconds as simply unusable. In online retailing, studies have even shown that shoppers drop off when response times exceed only one second. Because SOA makes use of the verbose **XML (Extensible Markup Language)** format and data is converted (marshaled and un-marshaled) when Web Services are called, overhead is generated. This abstraction places a performance tax on SOA applications.

The more services in a business process, the more vulnerable it is. If a business process depends on six data services, each of which achieves 99% uptime, the business process itself could have up to 6% downtime. That translates to as many as 525 hours of unplanned downtime each year. The problem doesn't end there. Although data services are designed for centralizing data access, scalability issues arise when many business processes depend on the same set of data services. On top of that, if IT is mandated to meet strict SLA agreements, it becomes extremely important to build SOA applications that perform on all RASP levels. But what is the best way to build a scalable data access store in the data tier? What is the best way to enable user applications, and in turn business processes, to quickly access data traditionally stored in databases?

In this chapter, we will discuss how a mid-tier caching strategy can inject high performance into data services as part of an SOA. We will also illustrate the approach a major pharmaceutical company undertook to improve the performance of a composite application using an Oracle Coherence Grid solution with Oracle SOA Suite.

SOA caching strategies

The performance of any SOA application is directly proportional to the amount of time it takes to retrieve the underlying data. Data within an SOA generally falls into one of two categories:

- **Service state**: This data pertains to the current state of the business process/service, that is, where the current process instance is at this point in time, which processes are active vs. closed vs. aborted, and so on. This data is particularly useful for long-running business processes, and is typically stored in a database to provide insulation against machine failures.

- **Service result**: This data is delivered by the business process/data service back to the presentation tier. Typically, this data is persistent and stored in backend databases and data warehouses.

Caching can play a very important role in improving the time taken to access service state or result data. Caching is used to minimize the amount of traffic and latency between the service using the cache and underlying data providers. In common with any caching solution, caching design for a business service must consider issues such as:

- How frequently the cached data needs to be updated

- Whether the data is user specific or application wide

- What mechanism to use to indicate that the cache needs updating, and so on

It is possible to cache both types of data—service state and service result.

- Service state caching allows you to share service state data between services in a business process in memory
- Service result caching allows you to cache results from frequently accessed business services or data services

The following figure shows how an SOA composite application can boost performance by caching data services and business services data:

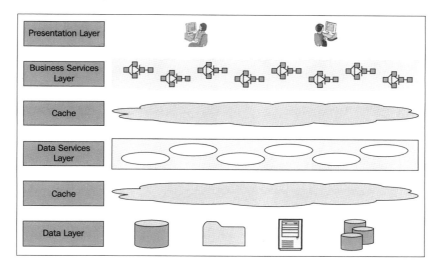

This is how the cache layers work:

- The upper cache layer caches both business service state as well as business service result (that is, results from the data service layer)
- The lower cache layer, in turn, caches both the data service state (if needed) as well as application data coming from underlying databases and applications

Let's understand how this works for the data services layer. The idea is to add the cache access immediately before the data source access by conditionally short-circuiting the data source access if there is a cache hit, and by adding a cache update after the data source access. The first time a service is called, the result is cached and served to the consumer. On subsequent calls, the application logic looks at the cache first and retrieves data directly from there, should it be available. This technique is called **cache-aside.**

The following figure illustrates how a composite SOA application can be architected for boosted performance by implementing caching at two layers:

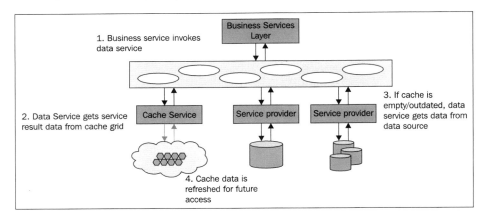

A cache-aside architecture can avoid expensive database access.

With data now located in memory in the middle tier, data access is much faster, enabling more intelligent services and faster response times. Basically, the primary goal is to avoid as many performance-degrading database accesses as possible by asking the question "*Does this information have to be real-time or is near real-time good enough?*" In the case where multiple invocations to a service over a short time are likely to return the same result, relaxing the requirement to near real-time data served from a cache will result in significant performance enhancements.

Cache-aside is an important performance-enhancing strategy, specifically for SOA applications that primarily read data from multiple different backend sources. A typical scenario involves assembling a 360-degree view of a customer across multiple data stores.

Cache-aside is common in the travel industry, where, for example, booking data is stored nearly in real-time in a cache. Allowing a database hit for every instance of someone browsing for hotel nights or airline seats would translate into scalability issues. Sometimes, this even requires a lookup in a third-party system, with each lookup resulting in a fee. Hence, most browsing for trips happens with near real-time data served from a cache. You can use the same technique to speed up your SOA application.

Providing a 360-degree customer view

A very large, research-based pharmaceutical company was challenged with customer information spread across multiple data stores. Additional backend systems had been added through geographic expansion and mergers and acquisitions on the business side. Customer information sat in multiple transactional CRM and ERP systems, in master data management stores, and in business intelligence data warehouses. This environment made it difficult to deliver a 360-degree view of a given customer, a view that reflected all the available information from past customer interactions. As a result, the company's sales force faced a constant struggle to get up-to-date information on customers (that is, physicians). Aggregating and filtering lists of information across multiple data sources for any given physician posed a significant challenge.

To further aggravate the problem, sales people needed real-time access to customer information, from anywhere. Imagine a scenario in which a sales representative is talking to a physician and has to recommend new products based on the physician's specialty, research, and buying pattern. A lack of information can seriously hamper the quality of the conversation, as well as the chance to up-sell/cross-sell. Hence, it was necessary that the new solution deliver a real-time experience to its sales force on their mobile devices.

The pharmaceutical company quickly realized it had to build an agile and fully configurable data integration solution to deliver a 360-degree view of the health care provider using a multi-channel SOA and Web 2.0-based solution presentation layer. This solution would successfully search for a customer across **Healthcare Project Management (HCPM)**, **Primary Care Case Management (PCCM)**, and marketing/campaign management applications (UNICA) and CRM (Siebel), Finance (Oracle E-Business Suite), Master Data Management (Siperian), and several other data sources.

Solution using Oracle SOA Suite and Oracle Coherence

This solution was architected to build a **Get Customer Activity (GCA)** composite application which provided the following features:

- Initiate and retrieve data from multiple data sources concurrently

- Return a list of candidate customers based on search criteria

- Select a customer from the candidate customer list and return an aggregated and filtered set of activity information specific to that candidate customer across multiple data sources (Betsy, USDW, and PubMed)

- Select a customer activity to view activity detail and return activity information (detail specific) about the customer
- Limit user visibility to data based on entitlement criteria (activity, channel, and territory)
- Return phonetically matched data

The following figure shows a GCA composite application displaying consolidated customer information:

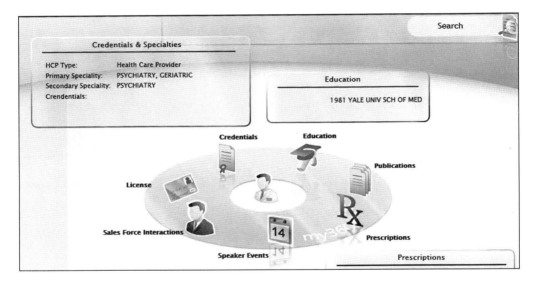

The pharmaceutical company selected Oracle SOA Suite for process and data integration and Microsoft SharePoint to provide a Web 2.0 layer to deliver the end information to the sales representatives.

The company also decided to pursue a caching strategy as a performance boost for SOA data services. However, the solution would have to be capable of meeting three important caching needs:

- The solution would have to accommodate a data-service cache size that could easily exceed the memory available on one box.
- In anticipation of gradual, global adoption, the solution would have to be capable of linear scalability through the addition of servers to the distributed cache.
- The solution would have to leverage the existing set of commodity servers in the company's SOA mid-tier in the most efficient manner possible for caching.

In short, the company needed a solution that could combine RAM memory available across multiple heterogeneous servers into a distributed shared memory pool. Based on these requirements, the company selected Oracle Coherence to distribute service data across multiple heterogeneous servers and coordinate that data across nodes in the clustered cache.

The following figure shows a GCA composite application using Oracle SOA Suite and Oracle Coherence:

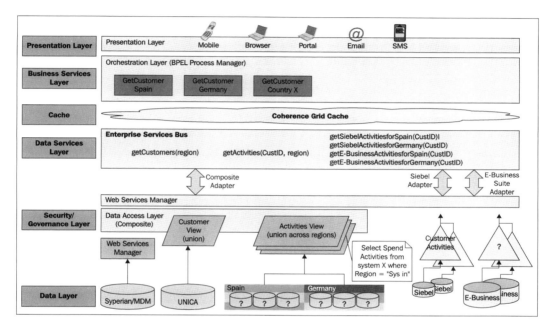

The GCA composite application provides important information on a specific customer activity through the following process:

1. Oracle BPEL PM orchestrates business services (**GetCustomer Spain, GetCustomer Germany**, and so on).

2. The business services invoke Oracle ESB data services (`getActivities`, `getCustomers` by region, `getCustomerActivity` by applications).

3. The data services in turn extract required data (through the security and governance layer) from relevant data sources (Siebel, UNICA, Siperian, and so on) and return the data back to Oracle BPEL PM.

4. Oracle BPEL PM eventually surfaces the result to the sales representative on a SharePoint portal.

The following figure shows the getCustomers (Germany) process flow:

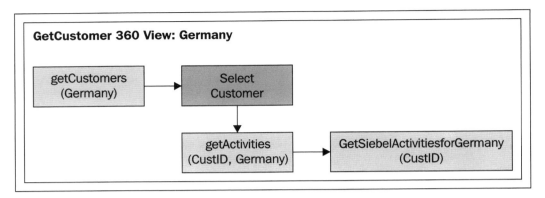

The speed at which the data is delivered to the sales representative's PDA depends on the speed at which the data services can retrieve data from the underlying data layer. Let's examine the role Oracle Coherence plays in this process.

BPEL: Coherence integration architecture

Within the GCA composite application, Oracle Coherence is used to cache the data service results data. Since this data doesn't change frequently, Oracle Coherence serves the data from memory rather than from the data source via a database call.

The following figure shows the interaction between BPEL PM, Coherence, and ESB:

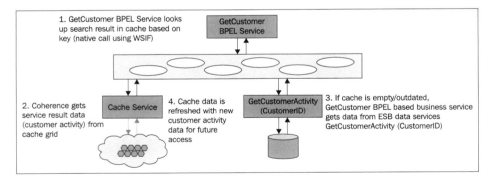

The previous figure illustrates the sequence flow between BPEL PM, Coherence, and ESB for extracting customer activity information. GetCustomer is a BPEL-based business service. Such business services would typically call the GetCustomerActivity data service (at the ESB layer), which in turn extracts the required data from underlying data services.

But since Coherence is used for caching the result data from the ESB data service, the sequence is a bit different. The first time the GetCustomer service is called, the result from `GetCustomerActivity` is cached and served to the consumer. On subsequent calls, the `GetCustomer` BPEL service looks at the cache first, and retrieves data directly from there (should it be available). Caching CustomerActivity data in memory in the middle tier boosts data access speeds.

How exactly should Coherence be used from BPEL, the SOA orchestration language? Given that the pharmaceutical company's goal for using mid-tier caching was scalable performance, the architecture should not compromise efficiency. Oracle Coherence offers a Java API; a native service call from BPEL to Coherence was a preference over a standard Web Service interface. The performance overhead of invoking Web Service operations is several orders of magnitude larger than that of invoking native Java classes. That's because marshaling and un-marshaling XML, processing SOAP envelopes, and so on are expensive operations.

The following figure shows a refined approach with WSIF Binding:

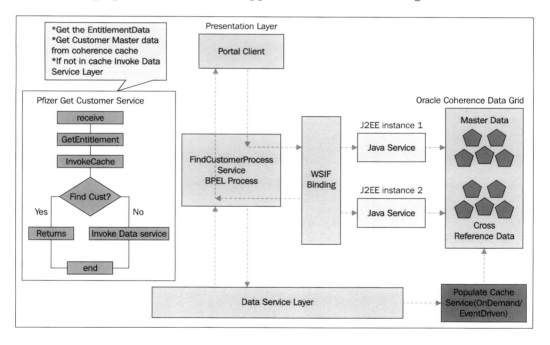

Native connectivity to Java resources is not a standard feature of BPEL, but Oracle BPEL **Process Manager (PM)** offers a solution for this purpose—**Web Services Invocation Framework (WSIF)**. WSIF requires no modifications or extensions to BPEL code. A detailed description of how to use WSIF with Oracle BPEL Process Manager is available in the Oracle BPEL Cookbook. In tests, we have experienced order-of-magnitude performance improvements leveraging WSIF bindings over standard Web Service interfaces to Oracle Coherence.

Integrating Oracle BPEL PM with Oracle Coherence

Let's take a quick look at the `GetCustomer` BPEL process. In the following figure, which shows the BPEL PM Process (GetCustomer) calling the Coherence cache, the process first checks the cache (also see Condition shown in the next to next screenshot). If the cache is empty, the process calls the underlying data service; otherwise, the results are returned from the cache.

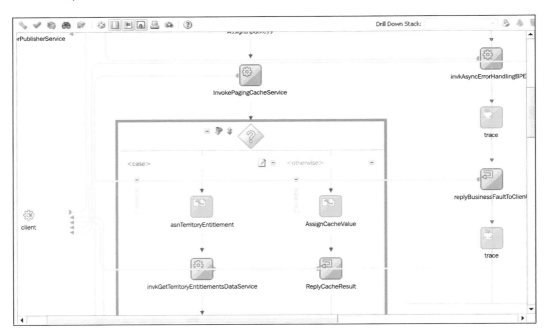

Partner links define how different entities (in this case the Coherence Web Service) interact with the BPEL process. Each partner link is related to and characterized by a specific `partnerLinkType` as shown in the following figure:

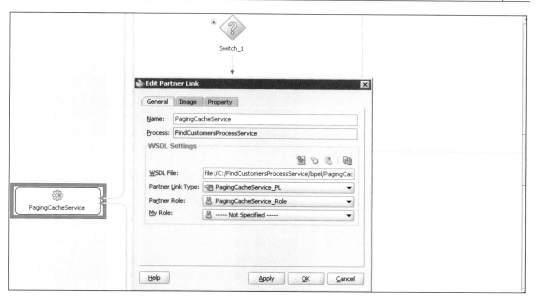

InvokePagingCacheService internally calls the Coherence WSIF Web Service. PartnerLinkType is defined in the WSDL file.

The following figure illustrates how the conditional expression is defined based on the value of the cache retrieved from `PagingCacheService`:

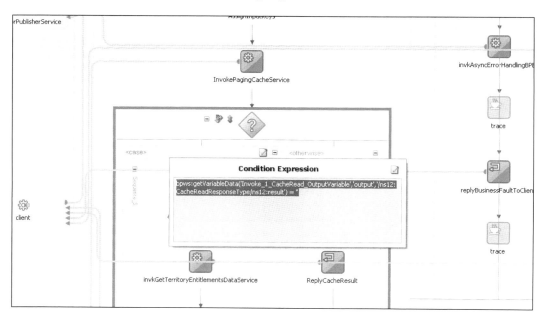

Now that we've seen how a BPEL process invokes the Coherence cache service, let's look at how this cache service is created. Briefly stated, the process involves creating a Java application that will read from, or write to, the cache. We then wrap this Java application as a Web Service to be called from the BPEL process.

From an implementation perspective, the following steps are necessary:

1. Create the Schema for request and response and WSDL for the cache service.
2. Create Java objects from the schema.
3. Create the Java implementation class for the cache service.
4. Create `coherence_config.xml` to configure Coherence.
5. Package `coherence.jar` and `tangosol.jar` within BPEL JAR.
6. Deploy and verify the process.

Step 1: Create the schema for request and response, and WSDL for the cache service

Because the BPEL process communicates with other Web Services, it relies heavily on the WSDL description of the Web Services invoked by the composite Web Service.

Depending on the customer schema, the search request and response schemas have to be prepared. For example, a customer search request will have first name, last name, search type, and so on. The response will have a list of customers, with each customer's address, purchased products, and so on.

The following figure shows the WSDL for the Coherence cache service:

```
                <part name="output" element="tns:CacheReadResponseType"/>
    </message>
    <portType name="PagingCacheServicePortType">
        <operation name="CacheWrite">
            <input message="tns:CacheWriteRequestType"/>
            <output message="tns:CacheWriteResponseType"/>
        </operation>
        <operation name="CacheRead">
            <input message="tns:CacheReadRequestType"/>
            <output message="tns:CacheReadResponseType"/>
        </operation>
    </portType>
    <binding name="PagingCacheServiceBinding" type="tns:PagingCacheServicePortType">
        <java:binding/>
        <format:typeMapping encoding="Java" style="Java">
            <format:typeMap typeName="tns:CacheWriteRequestType"
                            formatType="com.pfizer.www.ECRM.PagingCache.v1.CacheWriteRequestType"/>
            <format:typeMap typeName="tns:CacheWriteResponseType"
                            formatType="com.pfizer.www.ECRM.PagingCache.v1.CacheWriteResponseType"/>
            <format:typeMap typeName="tns:CacheReadRequestType"
                            formatType="com.pfizer.www.ECRM.PagingCache.v1.CacheReadRequestType"/>
            <format:typeMap typeName="tns:CacheReadResponseType"
                            formatType="com.pfizer.www.ECRM.PagingCache.v1.CacheReadResponseType"/>
        </format:typeMapping>
        <operation name="CacheWrite">
            <java:operation methodName="cacheWrite"/>
            <input/>
            <output/>
        </operation>
        <operation name="CacheRead">
            <java:operation methodName="cacheRead"/>
            <input/>
            <output/>
        </operation>
```

Step 2: Create Java objects from the schemas

Using schema (the utility bundled with SOA Suite), Java classes are created and then compiled.

Step 3: Create the Java implementation class to call Coherence

This is the Java application the BPEL PM service will call via the WSIF interface. Here's a quick snapshot of the Java code you'll need to read from the Coherence cache and return the results to the BPEL PM Service. The pertinent sections are highlighted.

```java
public class CacheServiceImpl {

    static NamedCache _customerQueryResultCache=null;
    static {
        /** Read coherence configuration file to initialize parameters
        like cache expiration, eviction policy **/

        System.setProperty("tangosol.coherence.cacheconfig",
        "coherence_config.xml");
```

```
   Thread thread = Thread.currentThread();
   ClassLoader loaderPrev = thread.getContextClassLoader();

   try
   {
      thread.setContextClassLoader(
          com.tangosol.net.NamedCache.class.getClassLoader());

      /** An instance of a cache is created from the CacheFactory
      class. This instance, called CustomerQueryResultCache, is
      created using the getCache() method of the CacheFactory
      class. Cache name GetCustomer.cache is mapped to a
      distributed caching scheme.**/

      _customerQueryResultCache =
                    CacheFactory.getCache("GetCustomer.cache");
       System.out.println("cache:
                    "+_customerQueryResultCache);

   }
   finally
   {

       Thread.currentThread().setContextClassLoader(loaderPrev);

   }
}
public CacheReadResponseType cacheRead(CacheReadRequestType input)
   throws ApplicationFault, SystemFault, BusinessFault
{

   String key = input.getInput().getKey();
   CacheReadResponseType cacheResponseType = null;

   /**A CustomerQueryResultCache is a java.util.Map that holds
   resources shared across nodes in a cluster. Use the key (in
   this case customer id) to retrieve the cache entry using the
   get() method) **/

   CustomerQueryResultSet customerQueryResultSet =
       (CustomerQueryResultSet)_customerQueryResultCache.get(key);
   System.out.println(" Requested key Id is : " + key);
   System.out.println(" Read from cache is : " +
       customerQueryResultSet);
   cacheResponseType =
       CacheReadResponseTypeFactory.createFacade();
   CacheReadResponse cacheResp =
       CacheReadResponseFactory.createFacade();
   if (customerQueryResultSet != null)
       cacheResp.setCustomerQueryResultSet(customerQueryResultSet);

       cacheResponseType.setResult(cacheResp);
```

```
            return cacheResponseType;

    }

}
```

Step 4: Create coherence_config.xml to configure Coherence

Now let's set up the caching configuration, including eviction policy and cache expiration. We'll use the distributed cache with expiry set to 0, so that the cached data never expires. Otherwise, we would be updating the cache when the data changes in the database.

```
<distributed-scheme>
  <scheme-name>default-distributed</scheme-name>
  <service-name>DistributedCache</service-name>
  <backing-map-scheme>
    <local-scheme>
        <scheme-ref>default-eviction</scheme-ref>
        <!-- Eviction policy set to LRU, so that least recently used
          cache data is evicted to make room for new cache -->
        <eviction-policy>LRU</eviction-policy>
        <high-units>0</high-units>
        <!--Expiry set to 0, so that the cached data never expires -->
        <expiry-delay>0</expiry-delay>
    </local-scheme>
  </backing-map-scheme>
</distributed-scheme>
```

The coherence_config.xml file should be put in a JAR file and added to the project libraries (refer to the following screenshot).

Step 5: Package Coherence.jar and Tangosol.jar within BPEL JAR

The `Coherence.jar` and `Tangosol.jar` files are now added to the project library, and get deployed with the BPEL JAR, which will come under `BPEL-INF/lib`, as shown in the following screenshot:

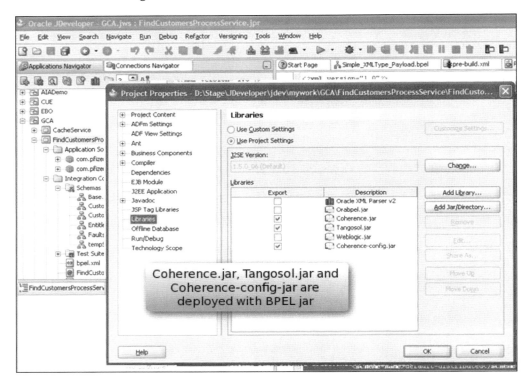

Step 6: Deploy and verify the process

Once the process is deployed and the first call is made, the process creates the `cacheserver` and creates the cache `getCustomer.cache`. This cache is mapped to the distributed caching scheme. From this cache instance, data is read or written.

Summary

By implementing mid-tier caching using Oracle Coherence, our composite application experienced significant benefits as shown in the following figure:

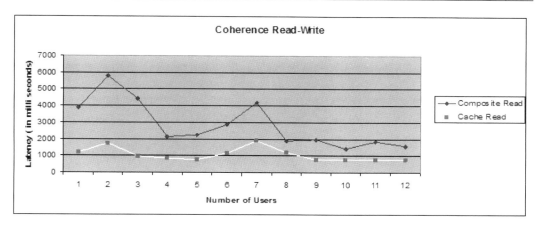

- Internal performance tests (refer to the previous figure) revealed response times that were 30% to 50% faster for data coming from cache. And since the data is closer to the Application server, it's easily available and avoids the database trip.

- Increased fault tolerance in the GCA composite application. Data is always available in the event of a failure of any single machine or server.

- Improved utilization of server hardware and more efficient use of server capabilities.

- Reduced data marshaling and un-marshaling during data service calls.

As this chapter has demonstrated, the use of sophisticated mid-tier caching solutions can improve the performance of SOA applications. A well-designed caching product shields the complex mechanics of a distributed and clustered cache, while allowing SOA architects/developers to focus on leveraging the cache. This results in additional benefits, including improved reliability through redundancy of the cache, and linear cache scalability from the shared-nothing architecture.

5

Integrated Real-time Intelligence with Oracle's WebCenter, Coherence, and Business Activity Monitoring

by Mark Farabaugh, Sri Ayyeppen, and Harish Gaur

Application users in today's world demonstrate an ever-increasing need for real-time intelligence as part of their user experience, as well as a variety of aggregate information (along with **Key Performance Indicators** in real time) when they need it, where they need it, and without having to search for it.

A bank teller processing transactions typically needs real-time intelligence for the customer in front of him. Without that information, the teller is in no position to offer sound advice on savings or changing investment patterns, or to advise them how to act on new information. This represents a lost opportunity to cross-sell and up-sell new products and services. If the bank teller had real-time intelligence on current mutual fund interest rates, the customer's investment pattern, and the health of the customer's investments, he could, for example, advise the customer to move funds from a low-interest account into a better-performing money market account for a short term.

However, intelligence alone is not sufficient. Once the intelligence is gathered, the next issue to address is accessibility. How does a user gain access to this critical data? Traditionally, many ways have been employed, including printed paper reports.

Traditional applications have always separated data entry or data management functions from reporting and analytics. They are handled by two different applications, two different information portals, or two different technologies.

Let's imagine the world of **Enterprise 2.0 (E2.0)**, in which every information worker is empowered to be a decision-maker, cutting out key bottlenecks upfront. In this scenario, nuggets of information are treated like gold and made available to the users when and where they need them. Why should business-critical analytical information be treated any differently? Users are constantly in need of these nuggets of **Business Intelligence (BI)**, as both historical and real-time information to help them create and manage their transactions much better.

A combination of BI and E2.0 allows us to combine information management and analytics in the same context and transaction. In this chapter, we will put together a reference architecture for contextual, real-time business insight. Using DJO as an example, a leading global provider of high-quality orthopedic devices, we will walk through a real-life example of how this is accomplished using Oracle WebCenter, Oracle Business Activity Monitoring, and Oracle Coherence.

Understanding real-time intelligence

So, what is real-time BI? To understand this, let's slide BI within an enterprise across three different categories:

- **Historical intelligence**: This is information aggregated over a period of years or months and typically stored in a data warehouse environment. Reports are run over minutes or hours to produce deep intelligence, collecting vast amounts of data.

- **Near-real-time intelligence**: This is data aggregated over the last few weeks or days, and typically stored in transactional databases. Information is produced by reporting tools querying these transactional databases.

- **Real-time intelligence**: This is information aggregated over the last few hours or days of data and typically stored in memory for fast access. Information is produced by analytical engines, and has short-term importance or relevance.

The need for real-time intelligence is becoming more critical. This is because traditional Enterprise Resource Planning applications and homegrown portals are focused mostly on transactions like creating an order, managing customer information, updating financial information, and so on. Gone are the days when transactions were viewed as a point of data management. You have to look at the process as a whole. The ability to create an order while you update customer and financial information during the transaction is critical. Businesses are grooming users to be decision-makers across a process in order to avoid a multi-step transaction process. As more and more businesses adopt this practice, real-time intelligence becomes key to any decision-making process.

Building a contextual, real-time BI application requires a combination of four key technologies—a Web 2.0 framework, **Business Activity Monitoring (BAM)**, grid caching, and a **Service-Oriented Architecture (SOA)**, as illustrated in the following figure:

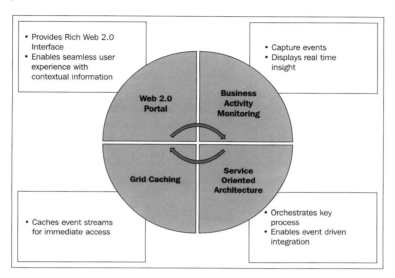

Let's run through these four areas.

1. **Web 2.0 Portal**: This portal provides content, presence, and social networking capabilities to create a highly interactive user experience. End users will use this portal to gain insight into real-time business activity.

2. **Business Activity Monitoring**: This will allow the application to capture key events occurring during a business activity. These events are aggregated, analyzed, and presented through a Web 2.0 Portal in easy-to-understand KPIs. Keep in mind that BAM is distinct from the dashboards used by BI. BI provides historical intelligence, whereas BAM processes events in real-time or near real-time.

3. **Service-Oriented Architecture**: This layer, along with the BAM layer, provides a platform for event-driven architecture. SOA is responsible for orchestrating the key business processes by integrating with a variety of enterprise applications. During the execution of processes, triggered events can be captured by the BAM layer, or services can be activated by triggers fired on incoming events. SOA and BAM integration typically takes place through the **Java Message Service (JMS)**.

4. **Grid Caching**: Data grid caching will boost the performance of the application by caching non-dynamic events into memory. This will eliminate the need for the Web 2.0 Portal to talk to the BAM/SOA layer for relatively static data and will provide extreme performance and scalability.

In the next section, we will put together a reference architecture and present an approach to build a contextual, real-time intelligence application.

Reference architecture

As previously discussed, this application requires integration between the Web 2.0 Portal, SOA, BAM, and a Grid Caching solution. The following illustration shows how these solutions come together:

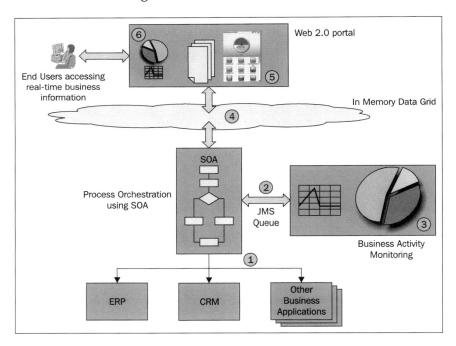

There are six steps in the processing sequence as shown in the following figure:

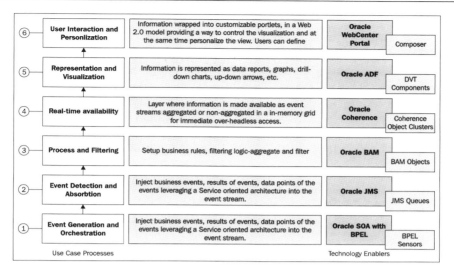

Let's dive into them, in greater depth:

1. **Event Generation and Orchestration**: All process activities requiring analytics are modeled through a loosely coupled orchestration process. This helps in efficiently altering the pattern (and any information captured) as part of the application event, if required. **Oracle BPEL Process Manager (BPEL PM)** can help here by allowing the user to model standards-based (BPEL) business processes. By using Oracle BPEL PM, an analyst can add activity sensors to monitor the execution of activities within a BPEL process, or add fault sensors to catch any failures. During this step, the process orchestration layer generates various events that are passed through JMS or a similar medium, and the **Enterprise Service Bus (ESB)**.

2. **Event Detection and Absorption**: The JMS bus provides the means to transport the events through a process into a BAM engine. The JMS messaging queue allows multiple endpoint systems to consume the business-generated events.

3. **Process and Filtering**: All the captured events are filtered, correlated, and analyzed to gauge their impact on critical KPIs and **Service Level Agreements (SLAs)**. The end user is notified of any new, pertinent information. The BAM engine continually updates the active report while it is being reviewed by the user. These updates continue until the user closes the report.

4. **Real-time availability**: BAM engines generally come with a built-in data cache. However, for large-scale enterprise solutions, there can be no trade-off between speed and scalability. In this situation, in-memory data caching solutions can significantly improve application performance. During this step, based on the frequency of data change, the data grid cache is refreshed and subsequent requests from the Web 2.0 portal are processed by the cache. Oracle Coherence provides this capability through an in-memory data grid layer that can cache as much as 1 TB of data. This approach not only improves application performance, but also makes the application less hardware intensive.

5. **Representation and Visualization**: During this step, the user is presented with visually powerful information. Developers can use declarative frameworks to model dynamic data objects to capture underlying intelligence. **Oracle Application Development Framework Data Visualization (ADF DVT)** components are a set of rich interactive Oracle ADF Faces components that provides significant graphical and tabular capabilities for visualizing and analyzing data.

6. **User Interaction and Personalization**: The Web 2.0 portal (Oracle WebCenter Portal) allows the user to aggregate a variety of information into a personalized dashboard. BAM charts, workflow activities from business processes, an interface to tweak KPIs, and the ability to define rules and filters all come together on a single screen. By providing additional integration and runtime customization options, control is placed directly in the hands of end users to slice, dice, and analyze data the way they want.

Now that we have reviewed the reference architecture and the six steps needed to build such an application, we will focus on the real-life implementation of a similar application at DJO Global.

Building a real-time call center application at DJO

DJ Orthopedics (DJO), headquartered in Vista, California, designs, manufactures, and distributes a line of technically advanced products and services for the prevention, treatment, and rehabilitation of acute and chronic orthopedic and spinal conditions. DJO, as part of its reimbursement business, runs call centers that process private and government medical insurance claims from all regions of the United States. The call centers also supply patients with healthcare devices and process the claims with insurance companies. Clinics and patients supply critical healthcare information as part of their claims. Call centers interact with healthcare insurance providers through **Electronic Data Interchange (EDI)** transactions.

Information about customers and orders is distributed across custom databases, third-party systems, and Oracle E-Business Suite. However, in this configuration, call center agents had no access to real-time aggregated customer information.

It is imperative for agents working on claim processing to view (in real time) the daily or weekly call activity associated with a specific claim. Call center managers require real-time forecasting and load distribution to process claims, recognize trends, and address cash flow.

In order to provide access to necessary information, DJO decided to build a real-time BI application that would support call center user interaction and showcase real-time information on:

- Call activity
- Order activity
- Financial activity
- Personal productivity goals

Case study architecture

DJO Global chose the combination of Oracle ADF, Oracle Coherence, Oracle BPEL PM, and Oracle BAM to build this solution, as shown in the following figure, with Oracle E-Business Suite at the core to provide all processes, from order management, contract management, fulfillment, and shipping to financials and order-to-cash.

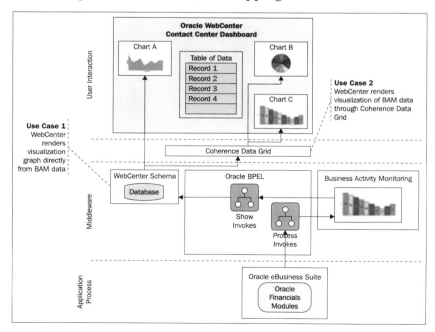

Let's review these architecture pieces using the invoice reconciliation DJO use case. DJO organizes all patient claims based on the insurance provider, and sends the claims invoices to the insurance companies for reimbursement. These external transactions are supported by business-to-business processes through Oracle SOA Suite. The insurance companies perform direct payment to the banks, and the banks send back EDI files to DJO with explanations of the payments. This information has to be reconciled with the source information sent to the insurance companies to ensure and sign off on records paid. If information cannot be reconciled, DJO processes records that are, for various reasons, not paid and marks them as pending reconciliation.

In some cases, pending transactions from past months may still be awaiting payment. There is a need for real-time intelligence as new files are received and new claims are adjudicated. It is necessary to get a real-time view of the records processed today, total records sent for reimbursement, total payments received, and records pending reconciliation.

As part of this reconciliation, multiple steps occur as follows:

1. Original source records are retrieved.
2. Source records are dispatched to insurance companies.
3. New payments are received and reconciled.
4. Agents are notified of claims that they need to process and finalize by working with the patients.
5. If paid by the insurance companies, information needs to be finalized in AR and receipts should be acknowledged.

Therein lies the need for a real-time dashboard that can be viewed by both call center agents and invoice agents so that they can collaborate, process, and rectify problems.

The following table details the design goals and solutions needed.

Design goals	Solution approach
Call center agents and invoice agents need visually rich dashboards to review invoice and order activity.	Leverage Oracle ADF DVT for visualization
Reconciliation information should be instantly available upon request (1000 transactions/second expected).	Oracle Coherence to act as in-memory data grid to collect and display data
Dashboards should be updated as soon as new reconciliation information is available. Agents should be able to analyze data in a variety of formats (charts, graphs).	Oracle BAM
The process of integrating order and invoice data should be automated. Processes and policies should be easy to adapt to new healthcare regulations.	BPEL engine as part of Oracle SOA Suite managed with Oracle BPEL PM

Now that we understand how all the pieces fit together in the context of the invoice reconciliation use case, let's walk through the six steps that were outlined earlier.

Step 1: Event generation and orchestration

As soon as new invoice reconciliation data is received, Oracle E-Business Suite triggers new events. Many Oracle E-Business Suite products leverage the Oracle Workflow Business Event System for business process integration. Although this is not the only method available for integrating Oracle E-Business Suite into a business process, it does allow an ESB or BPEL process to be event-driven using standard Oracle E-Business Suite functionality.

Oracle E-Business Suite posts real-time data to the *invoice monitor* BPEL process. An invoice schema (**XML Schema Definition**, or **XSD**) is created as a template for data validation from Oracle E-Business Suite.

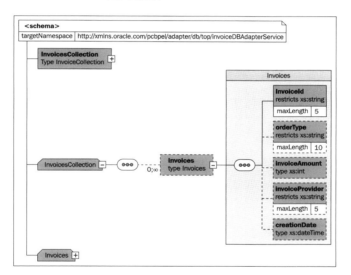

Leveraging the invoice XSD, the Oracle E-Business Suite event posts the data to the invoice monitor BPEL process for orchestration.

Step 2: Event detection and absorption

The invoice monitor BPEL process takes the invoice reconciliation data from Oracle E-Business Suite, enriches it, and sends it to the BAM layer. The following two figures offer two views of the invoice monitor process. The first figure is a **Service Component Architecture (SCA)** view of the BPEL process.

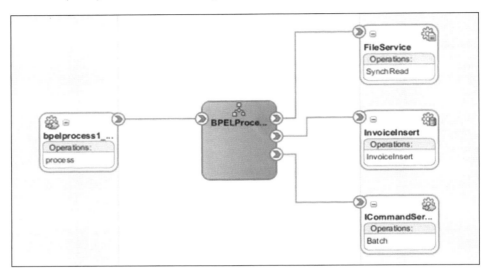

The second figure is a traditional view of the process, showing how it transforms data and sends it to BAM.

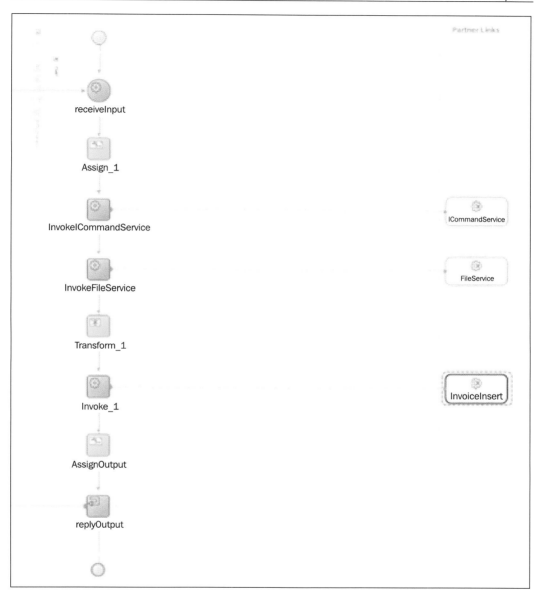

In this scenario, Oracle BPEL PM integrates with Oracle BAM using Oracle BAM Web Services. This can, alternatively, be done by sending the information on a JMS bus. Oracle BAM Web Services allow users to build applications that publish data to the Oracle BAM server for use in real-time charts and dashboards. Any client that can talk to standard Web Services can use these APIs to publish data to Oracle BAM.

The data objects in the Oracle BAM server are available using Oracle BAM Web Services and, in this case, using the **ICommand Web** service. An ICommand Web Service partner link is configured as shown in the following screenshot:

Once BPEL publishes this data to the BAM server, it is then processed and filtered.

Step 3: Processing and filtering

Oracle BAM receives invoice reconciliation data from the BPEL process and presents this data in the BAM dashboard with the help of invoice data objects. Invoice data objects reflect the business data that is captured in BAM for presentation, analysis, alerts, and so on. After execution of the invoice monitor BPEL process, an ICommand Web Service call populates the invoice data object.

In the following screenshot, you can see the definition of the invoice data object as well as the populated data:

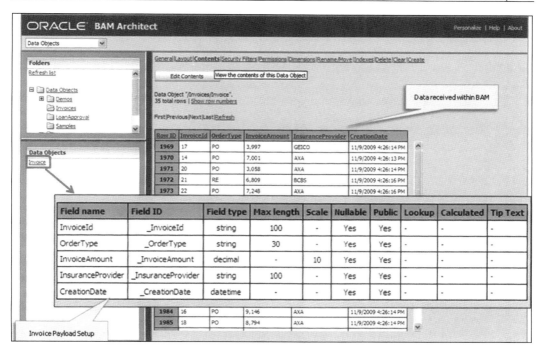

Filters help in limiting the subset of data and displaying the required business information. Filters can also be used to define certain KPIs or SLAs and display content matching (or which do not match) these criteria.

As shown in the following screenshot, data is filtered so that only invoice reconciliation data that is older than one week is displayed in the dashboard:

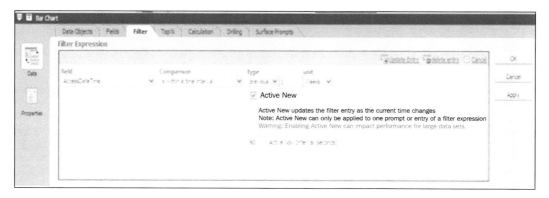

Once the data is stored and filtered, processed information is rendered live in the BAM dashboard. The Oracle BAM Architect process guides you in how to set up the charts and render the data in the dashboard.

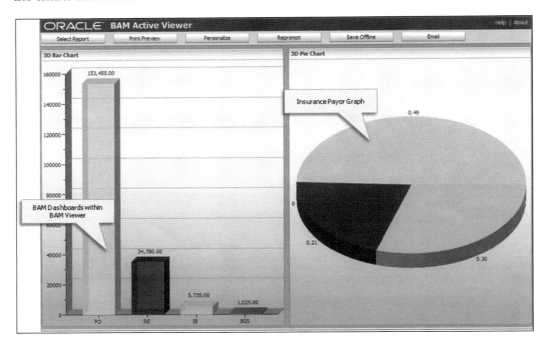

However, the BAM dashboard is not enough for invoice and call center agents. Agents want to see this information right within their dashboards as they are processing the patient or insurance company. So, in the next step, this information needs to be integrated into the overall dashboard.

Step 4: Real-time availability

The next step is to cache important BAM data in Oracle Coherence so that it can eventually be surfaced in the Oracle ADF user interface. Let's review how this is done.

A scheduled Store Invoices BPEL process retrieves the data from BAM and posts it to the Oracle database tables, as shown in the following figure:

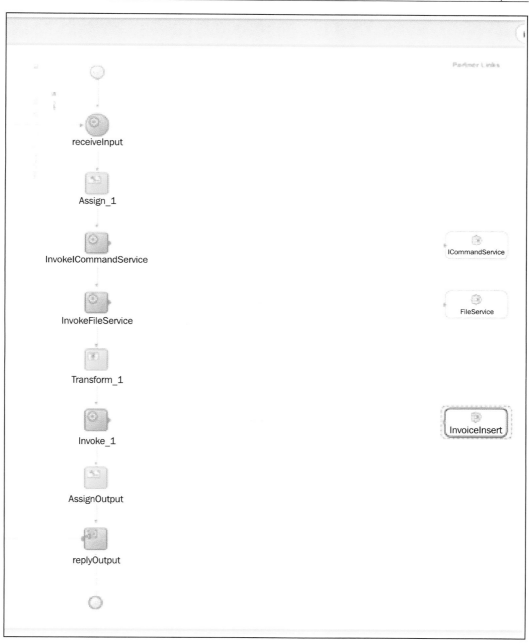

The Store Invoices BPEL process uses the ICommand Web Service to retrieve the data from the BAM data object to an XML file. After the `Invoices.xml` file is generated, it uses the file adapter service to retrieve the contents of the XML file.

The Store Invoices BPEL process then prepares a collection object comprised of all the invoice content present in the `Invoices.xml` file by using XSL transformation. Finally, it calls a PL/SQL procedure by passing the generated collection object. The PL/SQL procedure stores the data to the `Invoices` database table. It updates the existing records and creates a new record, if none already exists.

The next step is to configure the Oracle Coherence cache to reflect this data store for the application. The application is integrated with Oracle Coherence by configuring the application in Oracle JDeveloper. In Oracle JDeveloper, we refer to the Oracle Coherence cache configuration file with the workspace definition.

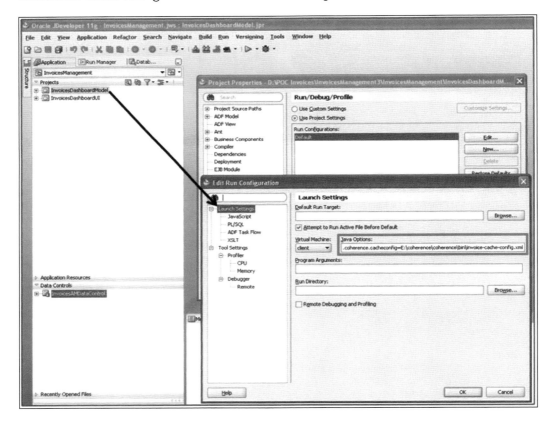

Add the following lines to the Java Configuration of the ADF Application:

- `Dtangosol.coherence.distributed.localstorage=false`
- `Dtangosol.coherence.log.level=3`
- `Dtangosol.coherence.cacheconfig=[ConfigLocation]\invoice-cache-config.xml`

With this logic, the information is now available to the Oracle ADF Model layer to be visualized with ADF View components.

For more information refer to Creating Oracle Coherence Caches in Oracle JDeveloper available at `http://www.oracle.com/technology/pub/articles/vohra-coherence.html`.

Step 5: Representation and visualization

Now we are ready to leverage the information available in the cache to render the information on a web application.

To enhance the visualization of the rendered event information in Oracle Coherence, we leverage the Oracle ADF DVT components that are available as part of Oracle ADF 11*g*. DVT components in Oracle ADF can be used to build graphical representations of data, such as bar charts, gauges, Gantt charts, and geographical maps. The best feature of DVT components is the declarative model in which the cache can be wrapped into a model layer as part of the Model-View-Controller pattern within Oracle ADF 11*g*. This model can help the view objects to hold real-time data, retrieved from the Oracle Coherence cache.

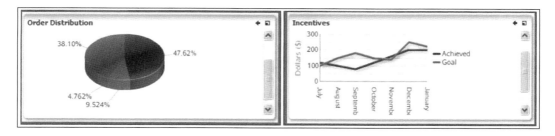

These charts are wrapped into an ADF task flow as reusable user interface components within a portal or an application. Task flow components are also made available to the Business Dictionary feature of Oracle WebCenter.

Step 6: User interaction and personalization

Now let's look at how these components are available for a user to interact with and personalize the data, as well as control the visibility of the information.

The dashboard in the following screenshot displays a view of the entire application. Invoice agents and call center agents get personalized views where different KPIs (work lists, orders, patient details, payees, patient notes, and physician details) come together. The result is a centralized view of their customers and an opportunity to have intelligent discussions with them.

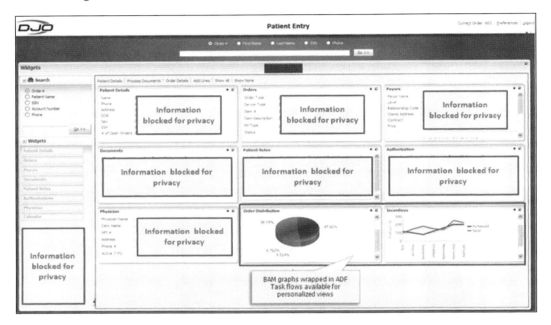

Summary

In this chapter, we learned that a contextual, real-time BI application requires a combination of four key technologies—a Web 2.0 framework, Business Activity Monitoring (BAM), grid caching, and Service-Oriented Architecture (SOA).

The combination of BI and E2.0 enables us to combine information management and analytics in the same context and transaction. This solution could easily evolve into an architecture that combines complex event processing with online analytical processing, to further expand the capabilities to leverage business intelligence.

6

Achieving Business Insight by Integrating Relational and Multi-dimensional Data

by Ross Sharman and Juliana Button

To establish competitive differentiation, organizations across the globe face similar issues—the need to simultaneously address situational questions ("What"), and forward-looking questions ("How"), as part of their everyday organizational reporting and planning needs. **Business Intelligence** (**BI**) solutions can help with the "What" analysis to provide past and present views of data and transactional reporting, whereas multi-dimensional **Online Analytical Processing** (**OLAP**) tools excel at "How" analysis, providing modeling and forecasting capabilities to determine how particular behavior will impact upon results. In the past, distinct BI solutions have addressed what really should be seen as a seamless BI continuum, as illustrated in the following figure:

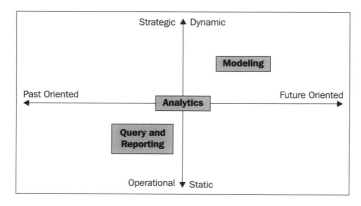

However, this transformation process can only happen if users can access data in the correct manner and format. These three data formats enable fast and effective data access to serve the three business purposes in the above diagram. Organizations in search of fast and flexible data analysis ultimately need a unified platform to do both. With this unified platform in mind, there are three key principles we believe are relevant for any BI integration project that seeks to leverage the benefits of a combined relational and OLAP foundation:

- A heterogeneous tool for data population to handle data input from a range of disparate physical devices and data stores
- A common enterprise information model that provides consistency, security, flexibility, and re-use
- Flexibility in reporting formats in order to accommodate the diverse needs of users across the BI continuum and rapidly changing reporting requirements

We'll discuss each of these in greater detail in this chapter.

Through the use of a real-world examples, this chapter highlights a compelling business need to integrate relational and multi-dimensional data. We will discuss how Australia-based Knowledge Global has used the combined power of BI and OLAP to build a carbon/energy monitoring and measurement application. Knowledge Global is a sustainability-focused company using their software enabler **EMMA (Environmental Management and Measurement Application)**, which allows sustainability measure and management. They detail resource consumption (water, gas, electricity, solid and liquid fuels, fertilizers, and so on) and report at the granular level of operations.

EMMA was conceived because it was recognized in 2001-2002 that the greatest challenge in the future will be the validation and verification of carbon emissions and carbon emission equivalents. It was also recognized that in order to manage carbon, it needed to be measured and quantified from point of source or the calculation would be invalidated, unverified, and false. There would be two reasons why this verification and quantification would be necessary:

- Because it was going to become the next form of currency
- Trade like the currency markets

CO_2 equivalents are not like money and manufactured in a controlled mint. CO_2e is created from the point of source, in many ways, from natural resource consumption, and from many sources. There needed to be a way to equate the use of resource with CO_2 and in turn to the value of the CO_2e in a trading market. In other words, a way to measure from point of source through to the trading market, calculated and converted along the way so the comparative analysis put apples with apples.

The only way this could be done was to combine leading technology with science. This is EMMA.

Integration architecture

Organizations can achieve significant, powerful insights and improved decision making by combining What and How analysis. The architecture employed to support this integration requires three important technologies, as shown in the following figure:

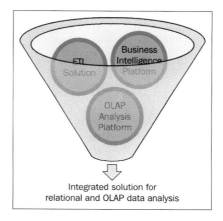

- An ETL tool to integrate data from disparate data sources and aggregate them into a common repository

- A Business Intelligence Platform to perform flexible reporting on relational data, and disseminate it to a variety of end users across different channels

- An OLAP Platform to enable business users to quickly model complex business scenarios to perform forecasting, discover trends, and understand behavior patterns

Let's take a look at key architecture best practices to build such a solution.

1st Principle: Integrate heterogeneous data population

Any BI integration project is all about data. With the rise of sensors and event-driven technology, businesses are generating and collecting significantly more data than ever before. So, the first challenge is to get all of the data into a manageable source repository, where it can be accessed, reported on, analyzed, and distributed.

Multiple BI repositories come into play when dealing with different data sources:

- OLTP to capture and store transactional operational data
- Data Mart/Data Warehouse to consolidate into multi-dimensional data
- OLAP for predictive modeling and forecasting

Data in these repositories could come from a variety of different data sources. An ETL tool helps load all these different repositories using data-based, event-based, or services-based integration. An integrated BI and OLAP environment can return strong dividends. A unified platform can enable Report to Source Lineage, that is, the ability to easily drill back from dashboard data to details about where the data came from and which transformations were applied.

2nd Principle: Build a common enterprise information model

BI and OLAP integration provides the ability to answer questions like "What is customer X's lifetime value for my enterprise?". To accurately answer such a question, it is important to have one enterprise definition for "lifetime value of a customer" across BI, OLAP, and other elements of the solution. A common enterprise information model is necessary to derive consistency, security, reuse, and flexibility across an integrated BI platform.

With an integrated BI platform, an end user could be looking at OLAP information, do a single click, and quickly navigate into the relational world. In this scenario, the end user is completely oblivious to the source of the information. The unified metadata model needs to serve all end-user tools, so every end user and every department has the same consistent view of information, tailored to each role. The model must account for all types of data sources that are assets of the enterprise, whether they are stored in relational or non-relational form. The model must also preserve the expressiveness of the data source. The following figure provides an illustration of how the different layers in data presentation and structure are used to perform specific business tasks.

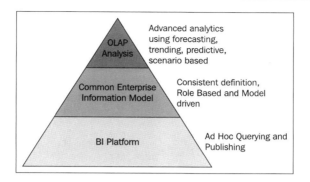

3rd Principle: Enable flexible reporting

How do you combine a sales revenue report (a "What" analysis) with a trend analysis showing how to improve sales in a particular region (a "How" analysis)? A flexible reporting and analysis framework is needed to address the diverse needs of different users across the BI continuum, from providing past historical views and present/current transaction and operational reporting to future-looking, predictive modeling, and analysis. A reporting platform should support Microsoft Office and Outlook integration so that modeling and forecasting can easily leverage this data. Support for reporting standards such as XBRL (a standards-based way to communicate business and financial information) can provide much needed flexibility.

Let's see how Knowledge Global used the power of OLAP, BI, and ETL, along with applying the principles outlined above, to build a carbon/energy management solution using **Oracle Business Intelligence Enterprise Edition** (**OBIEE**) and Oracle Essbase.

Energy efficiency management and monitoring with EMMA

With a growing global groundswell in the carbon/energy economy, Knowledge Global, a specialized consulting organization, wanted to develop an application that could help organizations measure, monitor, forecast, and reduce their carbon footprint. This application would help organizations answer "What" questions about past and present results including:

- Emissions and mandatory energy efficiency reporting
- Ability to spot trends and learn from past trends on energy consumption
- Verification of energy sources
- Quantification of energy/carbon reduction measures
- Validation of energy/emissions data reported

Also, in order to deliver a complete emissions solution, the application needed to address forward-looking "How" questions like:

- Energy efficiency/carbon reduction project viability
- Effectiveness of efficiency/carbon reduction strategies
- Carbon pricing and building asset modeling
- Modeling of renewable and alternative energy supplies
- Notifications and alerting for abnormal energy consumption
- Changing behaviors in the workplace
- Orchestrating and measuring efficiency projects

The solution required a combination of ETL, BI, and OLAP technologies to accurately report on operational data and provide modeling and forecasting capabilities.

EMMA architecture

Knowledge Global chose Oracle BIEE, Oracle Hyperion Essbase, and Oracle Data Integrator to build the EMMA.

The following diagram demonstrates how EMMA integrates data from various data sources (predominantly raw utility meter data) into the EMMA operational database (OLTP). Small queries can be issued onto the OLTP database but large cross-sectional queries will be inefficient and slow.

This very granular data is then summarized into a data mart structure that allows fast interrogation by the OBIEE toolset.

The data mart data set is further summarized into the OLAP database, which allows real slicing and dicing of the data at a macro level. All three databases are able to be queried through the same toolset (via the OBIEE semantic layer) allowing seamless integration for the user.

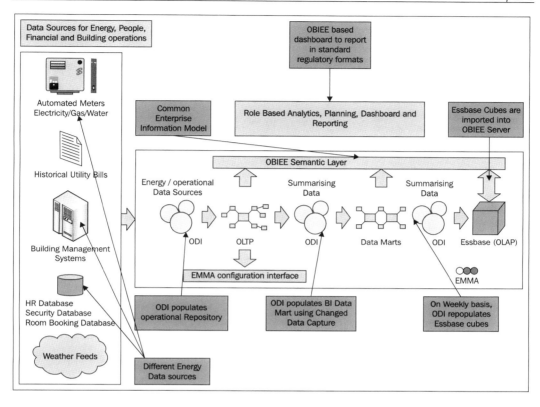

The three Oracle solutions do different things:

- **Oracle Data Integrator** (**ODI**) is an ETL tool, used to aggregate data from energy sources like smart meters, security systems, electrical circuits, and so on

- **Oracle BIEE** is used to accurately report on energy measurements in standard formats prescribed by the UN, industry, and governmental bodies

- **Oracle Essbase** is an analytical OLAP Engine. Essbase is employed to plan for the future through modeling and predictive forecasting and to help mitigate carbon exposure and maximize potential revenue

Let's quickly review three important aspects of this architecture.

Heterogeneous data population

The solution deals with a multitude of data formats. Data comes from smart meters for electricity usage, the Bureau of Meteorology for weather details, the Building Security System for personnel traffic, and various other systems.

This data flow ranges from the most granular operational data-store level (measuring isolated devices and events in seconds), to the data-mart star schema structure (measuring rooms and energy circuits, at a minimum of minutes but typically hours), and finally to Essbase OLAP (where we measure buildings and demographic groups, and in months).

The EMMA environment uses **Oracle Data Integrator (ODI)** to capture data from these different energy data sources and load data into appropriate BI stores, including the EMMA operational store, the star schema data mart, and the Essbase OLAP repository.

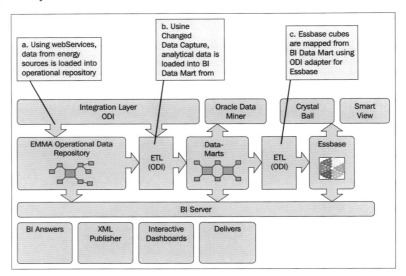

ODI uses Web Services for collecting data from internal data sources, such as Smart meter data, as well as external data sources, such as weather and forecast data. For example, the weather data and forecasts are obtained by a custom Web Service, which is wrapped around public websites. The output is XML data, which, using ODI, can be populated directly into the EMMA repository. On the other hand, integration with the Building Security System is file-oriented. The Building Security System exports data into comma-delimited files, which are mailed and copied to a processing directory. ODI processes files in this directory and loads them into the operational data store. Let's cover the dataflow sequence.

- **Energy Data Sources to Operational Data Store (EMMA Database)**: ODI is scheduled at regular intervals to process these files and Web Services, and then populate the data into the EMMA database via staging tables, adhering to a few business and validation rules. The data is then populated into the EMMA repository, applying several business rules (defined as knowledge modules) around this transformation to ensure the data is clean.

- **EMMA Database to BI Data Mart**: The data is then consolidated into the data marts on a nearly constant basis, ensuring that the analytics layer is up to date. ODI uses Changed Data Capture in the EMMA OLTP database to determine the data to be copied into the data marts. There is typically minimal information change on the data mart dimensions, with the majority of changes coming from the meters, which is an accumulation of electricity and carbon data on an hourly basis.

- **BI Data Mart to Essbase**: On a weekly basis, ODI is scheduled to re-populate the Essbase cubes, for planning and high-level analytics. We used the ODI adapter for Essbase, which makes mapping to the target cubes a straightforward process. The data granularity in the Essbase cubes is on a monthly basis. Data load problems in any of the three ELT processes are logged by ODI, and automatically flagged to the administrators, who can then attend to the errors.

Common enterprise information model

The data from all three of our data sources (EMMA OLTP, EMMA Data Mart, and EMMA Essbase OLAP model) is exposed through Oracle's BI Enterprise Edition interface.

The BI Repository stores the business intelligence metadata that is rendered inside the BIEE reports, Interactive Dashboard clients, and other clients. How is data represented in uniform fashion without any dependency on underlying data sources or presentation clients? Flexibility comes from a separation between presentation, logical, and physical data. The BI Repository defines three layers of abstraction—Physical, Business Model and Mapping, and Presentation. The Physical layer contains information about the physical data sources to which the BI Server submits queries. This physical layer gives us the ability to query analytical data coming from the BI Data Mart and multi-dimensional OLAP data coming from the Essbase cubes. The Business Model Layer, in turn, brings together data elements from the BI Data Mart and Essbase into a logical Star-Schema representation, creating uniformity in common enterprise definitions.

To integrate the Essbase OLAP data, we imported Essbase cubes into the Physical layer of the BI Repository using the BI Administration tool. The Essbase cube corresponds directly to our business model, so creating the Business Model and Mapping layer was easy because the metadata was implied by the structure of the Essbase cube. The following screenshot shows the BI Administration tool in which the semantic layer is defined; it shows how the multi-dimensional OLAP data structure is easily imported.

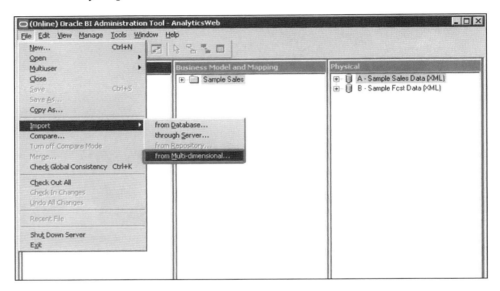

Full step-by-step instructions for this are provided in the tutorial, Integrating Oracle Essbase with Oracle Business Intelligence Suite Enterprise Edition (http://www.oracle.com/technology/obe/obe_bi/bi_ee_1013/essbase/biee_essbase.htm).

With this seamlessly integrated architecture, the highly consolidated data in the Essbase OLAP data sources can be drilled down into, to provide lower levels of granularity as stored in the data marts, and even down to the EMMA operational data store.

Flexible reporting

Dashboards are used to align figures from all three of our data repositories—planning (targets and budgets), data marts for business intelligence and real time for alerting, and business rules against operational data.

Because carbon has become a financial entity, there will be requirements to submit and receive financial information (including budgeted emissions and the proposed steps to mitigate these emissions). With the seamless integration between Essbase and BIEE, this type of information can come straight from the planning cube via the BI Server. The BI Server has interfaces through Web Services and BI Publisher to fit any (XML-based) reporting methodology that fits the XBRL reporting structure. The following diagram demonstrates the continuous improvement cycle within an environment using EMMA. The raw energy data measures pass through the three repositories and serve different purposes in the carbon reporting and management lifecycle. Data is displayed via dashboards for analytical purposes and the display of energy and carbon benchmarks. These benchmarks are used to help influence behaviors within the workplace (via orchestrated awareness projects). The EMMA reporting mechanism is used to fulfill mandatory and voluntary emission reporting, which are becoming more commonplace now. Finally, the planning perspective closes the loop of improvement by creating and modeling future scenarios.

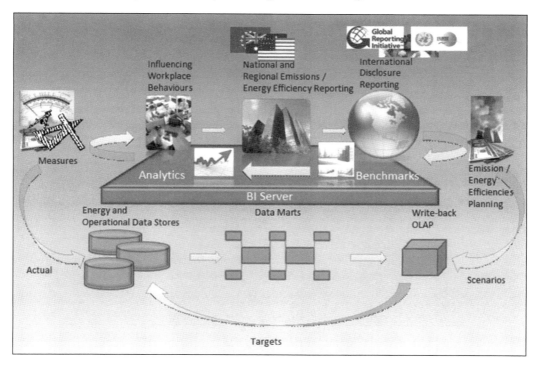

University energy efficiency management

Now that we have seen the EMMA architecture, let's walk through a specific example in which the EMMA application has been put into practice. This will help you visualize how data varies across three different EMMA data stores and what the final dashboard looks like.

The example is based on a large university that occupies in excess of 400 large multi-storied buildings. One CBD building has been selected for this example and a number of floors were examined in detail. Within this building, two very different groups, members of the student computer laboratory and university administration staff, operate on two floors.

We grow our understanding of the two occupant groups by measuring the consumption of energy (95% of which is electricity) on each of these two floors using two electrical sub-meters. For example, we can measure consumption against the security system to find out when people are on these floors, and/or we can measure the consumption against student and staff timetabled space occupancies. In this manner we can slowly build profiles of energy consumption for occupant group traffic for various floors of the building. These behavioral profiles then provide the basis for new energy-efficient initiatives to reduce consumption. These initiatives can be profiled using the scenario capabilities in Essbase to determine their effectiveness.

In general, the majority of electricity consumption on each floor across the entire building is created from air conditioning, ventilation, lighting, and personal computers. The lighting on each floor is manually switched on or off by people as they enter or exit the floor. The air conditioning, however, is automatically triggered when people enter the floor. Therefore, one person can incur a cost of tens of dollars by working alone. This illustrates where accountability and behavioral changes can create efficiencies.

In the example, we see that the students operate at very different hours as compared to the administration staff, often working through the night. However, the fact that one or two students choose to work in the early morning makes this a very inefficient use of energy per person. An education program to inform the students why this use of energy is inefficient is introduced, resulting in increasing awareness and a greater degree of accountability. This education initiative will be backed up with a security initiative to close the labs from 10:00 pm to 8:00 am during the week. All students have laptops, which means other working options are available. Students are also a demographic group that is keen to be a part of efforts to reduce energy consumption. The financial savings of this initiative can be modeled using the OLAP database.

Step 1: Data from meter and security systems

The meter data shown next illustrates the data coming in from the smart meters that monitor electricity usage for the whole floor (that is, lighting, air conditioning, and circuits). This information is logged at 15-minute intervals. There is also an hourly feed from the security system that logs people coming and going, so we can derive an average number of occupants for each hour.

Ref	Meter ID	Timestamp	KwH
10014	T0000241	5/05/2009 3:15	0.188
10014	T0000241	5/05/2009 3:30	0.188
10014	T0000241	5/05/2009 3:45	0.188
10014	T0000241	5/05/2009 4:00	0.188
10014	T0000241	5/05/2009 4:15	0.125
10014	T0000241	5/05/2009 4:30	0.125
10014	T0000241	5/05/2009 4:45	0.125
10014	T0000241	5/05/2009 5:00	0.062
10014	T0000241	5/05/2009 5:15	0.125
10014	T0000241	5/05/2009 5:30	0.188
10014	T0000241	5/05/2009 5:45	0.188
10014	T0000241	5/05/2009 6:00	0.062
10014	T0000241	5/05/2009 6:15	0.125
10014	T0000241	5/05/2009 6:30	0.062
10014	T0000241	5/05/2009 6:45	0.125
10014	T0000241	5/05/2009 7:00	0.125
10014	T0000241	5/05/2009 7:15	0.062
10014	T0000241	5/05/2009 7:30	0.125
10014	T0000241	5/05/2009 7:45	0.062
10014	T0000241	5/05/2009 8:00	0.125
10014	T0000241	5/05/2009 8:15	0.062
10014	T0000241	5/05/2009 8:30	0.375
10014	T0000241	5/05/2009 8:45	0.312
10014	T0000241	5/05/2009 9:00	0.188

Building	University Building, Campus A	University Building, Campus A	University Building, Campus A	University Building, Campus A	University Building, Campus A	University Building, Campus A	University Building, Campus A
Date	5/05/2008	5/05/2008	5/05/2008	5/05/2008	5/05/2008	5/05/2008	5/05/2008
Time	3:00	4:00	5:00	6:00	7:00	8:00	9:00
Floor	12	12	12	12	12	12	12
Current Occupants	0	0	0	0	10	2	8

Step 2: EMMA OLTP data structure

By consolidating and combining the raw meter data with the raw security system data, the EMMA OLTP system provides a real-time view of how electricity consumption is dictated by personnel operations.

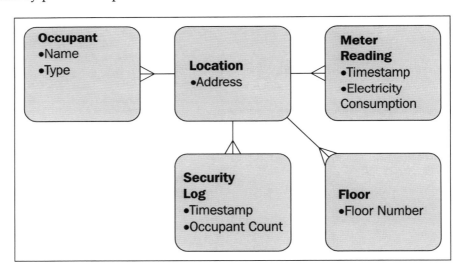

Basic OLTP design does not allow for time series analysis of large sets of data. However, utilizing this data source is important for verifying information at the most granular level. You can roll up from this level to the data mart.

Building Operator	University Property Services	University Property Services	University Property Services	University Property Services
Location	Floor 12, University Building, Campus A	Floor 12, University Building, Campus A	Floor 12, University Building, Campus A	Floor 12, University Building, Campus A
Floor Tenant	Student (School of Economics)	Student (School of Economics)	Student (School of Economics)	Student (School of Economics)
Date	5/05/2008	5/05/2008	5/05/2008	5/05/2008
Time	3:00	4:00	5:00	6:00
Electricity Usage (kwh)	17	12	12s	12
Occupants	2	0	0	0
Meter ID	T0000241	T0000241	T0000241	T0000241

Building Operator	University Property Services	University Property Services	University Property Services
Location	Floor 12, University Building, Campus A	Floor 12, University Building, Campus A	Floor 12, University Building, Campus A
Floor Tenant	Student (School of Economics)	Student (School of Economics)	Student (School of Economics)
Date	5/05/2008	5/05/2008	5/05/2008
Time	7:00	8:00	9:00
Electricity Usage (kwh)	14	18	22
Occupants	0	2	8
Meter ID	T0000241	T0000241	T0000241

Step 3: EMMA data mart structure

The EMMA OLTP data is then consolidated into the data marts, where trends and benchmarks can be derived. Here, we can profile the energy usage per person type for a particular building floor. The benchmarks can be modeled over many floors and buildings to help model the complete picture of the university's energy consumption and identify efficiency opportunities.

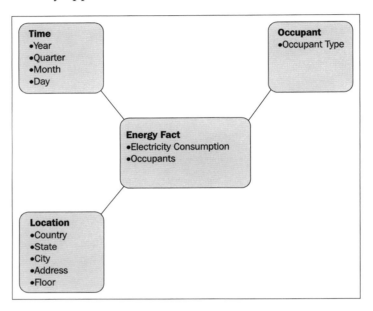

The data mart consolidates OLTP data into a format where measurements can be analyzed by different dimensions at different levels. This also allows time series analysis (that is, trending) to be performed. From the dashboards you can drill down from this level to the OLTP source for the originating values, or roll up to the OLAP level to allow broader (and faster) analysis and forecasting.

Dimensions	Hierarchy/Level	Attribute	Value	Value	Value	Value
Demographic	Faculty	Faculty	School of Economics	School of Economics	School of Economics	School of Economics
	Group	Group	Student	Student	Student	Student
Building	Country	Country Name	Australia	Australia	Australia	Australia
	State	State Name	NSW	NSW	NSW	NSW
	Campus	Campus	Campus A	Campus A	Campus A	Campus A
	Building Name	Building Name	University Building	University Building	University Building	University Building
	Floor	Floor Number	12	12	12	12
Date	Year		2008	2008	2008	2008
	Quarter		2	2	2	2
	Month		May	May	May	May
	Day		5	5	5	5
	Hour		8:00	9:00	10:00	11:00
Energy Fact		Kwh	18	22	28	32
		Occupants	7	8	8	8

Step 4: EMMA OLAP data structure

The OLAP cube consolidates the data mart into a MOLAP model that allows quick ad-hoc analysis, high-level trend analysis, and forecasting. From the dashboards you can drill down on consolidated figures for more detail in the data mart or even OLTP levels.

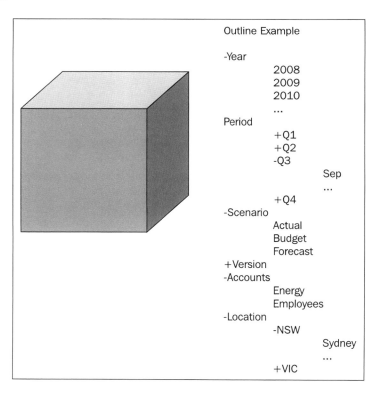

We can then use these benchmarks for projections using the EMMA OLAP Model. Here we profile the typical usage of the two groups during a working day and then observe the savings if forced closure of the student lab occurs from 10:00 PM to 8:00 AM. The students can be educated with this reasoning by demonstrating to them the cost per person of a few night owls working all hours (highlighted in the following screenshot). When accumulated across all student labs across the university over a year, the savings can be very worthwhile.

	Budget	Budgeted electricity cost by floor for student																							
Student Profile	Scenario 1																								
Monday																									
	Hour	1:00	2:00	3:00	4:00	5:00	6:00	7:00	8:00	9:00	10:00	11:00	12:00	13:00	14:00	15:00	16:00	17:00	18:00	19:00	20:00	21:00	22:00	23:00	0:00	TOTAL
University Building	Floor 12																								
Actual Average Occupants (2008)		2.00	2.00	1.00	1.00	1.00	1.00	2.00	4.00	8.00	16.00	18.00	20.00	24.00	28.00	22.00	22.00	20.00	15.00	13.00	12.00	8.00	4.00	2.00	2.00	
Actual Average Kwh		19.00	18.50	16.00	16.00	17.00	12.00	17.00	18.00	20.00	22.00	26.00	28.00	34.00	38.00	34.00	30.00	26.00	24.00	22.00	22.00	20.00	19.00	19.00	19.00	536.50
Actual Average Cost ($0.10/kwh)		1.90	1.85	1.60	1.60	1.70	1.20	1.70	1.80	2.00	2.20	2.50	2.50	3.40	3.80	3.40	3.00	2.60	2.40	2.20	2.20	2.00	1.90	1.90	1.90	53.65
Actual Cost/Person		0.95	0.93	1.60	1.60	1.70	1.20	0.85	0.45	0.25	0.14	0.14	0.14	0.14	0.14	0.15	0.14	0.13	0.16	0.17	0.18	0.25	0.48	0.95	0.95	
Budget Average Occupants (2009)		0.00	0.00	0.00	0.00	0.00	0.00	0.00	4.00	8.00	16.00	18.00	20.00	24.00	28.00	22.00	22.00	20.00	15.00	13.00	12.00	8.00	0.00	0.00	0.00	
Budget Average Kwh		0.00	0.00	0.00	0.00	0.00	0.00	0.00	18.00	20.00	22.00	26.00	28.00	34.00	38.00	34.00	30.00	26.00	24.00	22.00	22.00	20.00	0.00	0.00	0.00	364.00
Budget Average Cost		0.00	0.00	0.00	0.00	0.00	0.00	0.00	1.50	2.00	2.20	2.50	2.50	3.40	3.50	3.40	3.00	2.60	2.40	2.20	2.20	2.00	0.00	0.00	0.00	36.40
Budget Cost/Person		0.00	0.00	0.00	0.00	0.00	0.00	0.00	0.45	0.25	0.14	0.14	0.14	0.14	0.14	0.15	0.14	0.13	0.16	0.17	0.18	0.25	0.00	0.00	0.00	
Budget Saving $'s		1.90	1.85	1.00	1.00	1.70	1.20	1.70	0.00	0.00	0.00	0.00	0.00	0.00	0.00	0.00	0.00	0.00	0.00	0.00	0.00	0.00	1.90	1.90	1.90	$ 17.25

Step 5: Consolidated dashboards

In this simple example, you can see the power of combining the data at different roll-up levels and applying predictive modeling and forecasting, and how this can aid planning and budgeting to ensure the most efficient energy usage. Of course, this data is best displayed visually, on the OBIEE dashboards, as shown in the following screenshot:

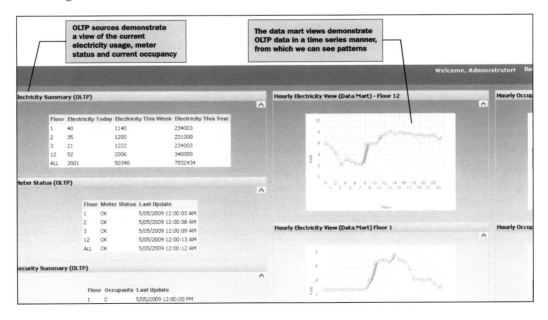

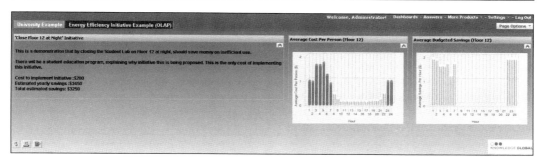

The previous screenshot demonstrates the modeling example in the OLAP data set. We can show "Why" (areas circled) and "How" the savings will be achieved. This data can be used to show any budgeted costs associated with this initiative and also the total expected savings. Of course, the real benefit of an OLAP model is the way such small budgets can be rolled up to a larger projected budget over the whole university.

This chapter has illustrated how the EMMA application can be put into practice at a university to accurately report, monitor, and mitigate carbon exposure. From a development perspective, the EMMA roadmap includes opportunities for:

- Expanding the underlying Service-Oriented Architecture to leverage the Oracle Service Bus for real-time integration, and Business Activity Monitoring for real-time alerting. Knowledge Global is also looking at Complex Event Processing to provide an additional level of intelligence to the vast amounts of streamed data.

- Oracle Governance, Risk, and Compliance Manager could be leveraged to achieve compliance with Australia's **National Greenhouse and Energy Reporting System** (**NGER**) and **Energy Efficiency Opportunities** (**EEO**) reporting, in order to avoid potentially significant fines for non-compliance.

- E-learning could help bring about behavioral change through employee interaction. Integrating an E-learning tool to EMMA will provide staff with a real-time, interactive view of how they can help reduce energy consumption at their workplace.

Summary

As organizations try to synthesize the vast amounts of data they are amassing to help deliver competitive advantage, they are increasingly turning to Business Intelligence solutions. Companies are recognizing that by augmenting their traditional operational using Business Intelligence tooling with multi-dimensional OLAP capabilities, they can cover the entire BI continuum to address both situational ("What") questions and forward-looking ("How") questions to help determine how a particular behavior will impact upon results. While building solutions to perform combined analysis, it is necessary to account for varying data formats, multiple repositories, and different presentation clients. A unified ETL, BI, and OLAP platform can provide the required level of integration between the different moving parts.

The authors wish to thank Juliana Button, Robin Hazel, and Alan Lee for their assistance in preparing this chapter.

7

Building Intelligent Processes with Insight-driven Agility

by Matt Miller and Mark Simpson

Business processes are part of the DNA of an organization. They enable the organization to deliver service to its customers, and execute the business model in a consistent way. As organizations change, their business processes have to change with them. Agility at this process level is essential—with a need to adapt quickly to changes in market conditions, regulatory requirements, or business models. A **Service-Oriented Architecture** (**SOA**) forms the foundation of process agility.

SOA enables business processes to be abstracted out of underlying application systems, yet work with the functionality of these internal and external assets to deliver more agile processes. Separating out the business rules and making them available as services for the business process to consume is a second key enabler for agility in SOA.

Learning to exploit this agility in the most effective way and manage the resulting business change poses an additional challenge to an organization. This business change is driven by strategic decision-making, by evolving and refining the business model, and by the tactical necessity to react to both internal and external unforeseen factors. Business insight delivered through a **Business Intelligence** (**BI**) toolset surfaces strategic and tactical business metrics with context to help make those decisions on how best to exploit the agility provided by the underlying SOA infrastructure.

Business processes that are supported by SOA allow the organization to directly execute the business model and better support business change; BI provides measures that inform decisions for strategic and tactical change within an organization. Combining SOA with BI allows you to act on those measures, changing processes, services, and rules to target identified improvement goals. SOA and BI are natural partners for a changing organization.

In this chapter, we will learn about three business drivers and corresponding architecture patterns for combining BI with SOA. We will then review how Motability Operations, the largest UK-based fleet operator, built an agile solution to drive a vehicle remarketing initiative using Oracle SOA Suite, Oracle BIEE, and Oracle Business Rules.

Business Intelligence meets Service-Oriented Architecture

BI has, for a long time, been associated with SOA as a complementary approach. However, this association has often only been focused at the boundaries of BI and SOA—using SOA Data Services and Events to provide information for a BI Reporting schema or utilizing BI tools to report on the usage and effectiveness of Business Services. The complementary nature of the two approaches goes even further, and substantial benefits can be realized by weaving BI and SOA together to deliver business solutions that are both agile and highly insightful.

Business patterns and architecture for combining BI with SOA

This chapter focuses on three key patterns for combining BI and SOA approaches to support business agility and meet the requirements of a changing business landscape. These patterns will form the basis of the use case introduced in the case study.

Actionable business insight

Actionable business insight uses information in BI dashboards to initiate SOA services that will take actions, such as moving loan profiles from one product to another, if the dashboards suggest that a particular product is unsubscribed. The key enabler for this business pattern is the identification of thresholds, and building them into your BI dashboards as guided alerts to identify business exceptions. These exceptions could be issues such as an overloaded call centre, or they could be opportunities such as identifying that a given call centre is performing exceptionally well for a particular type of product.

The first stage of actionable insight is to provide alerts and context to users to identify the need for actions, and then present links that will allow users to take those actions. These links will invoke business services that could be a simple data update, such as changing the default call centre, or they could be services that execute a business process, such as a call centre product transfer process. These business services could also change business rule parameters, such as reducing the rating that indicates that a customer is seen as high risk if the BI metric for current risk exposure goes above a certain threshold.

The second stage of actionable insight is to automate the triggering of an action. In this case, a dashboard is only used to support the automatic decision to invoke a business service that runs a process or changes a rule. The dashboard may be issued to a manager to review and monitor the results of the automated change, or it may just be recorded as a snapshot to feed process improvement or internal and external process audits.

The architecture pattern shown next identifies thresholds for the business metric, and invokes services that will execute a business process to exploit positive threshold breaches (and mitigate the damage done from negative threshold breaches). This architecture pattern turns an informative BI metric into an actionable BI metric by combining it with SOA services.

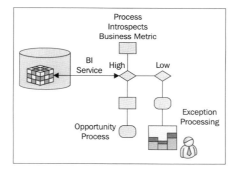

Insight-driven process

This allows SOA-driven business processes to introspect analytics through BI services to determine the path through which a process should be taken. For example, if a BI service shows that a particular branch is busy and not hitting conversion targets, the business process could route new loan applications to a branch with the capacity to fulfill the requests and generate a track record for the conversion.

While the first pattern changes rules and process paths reactively at runtime, based on an authorized BI alert, this pattern is built in at design time. The BI metric is available to the process modeler as a way to guide the path through the process. At design time, the business analyst considers multiple versions of the process, such as a high-risk customer acquisition process and a risk-averse version of the same business process.

The second architecture pattern allows BI metrics to be used in a business process or decision service, or to be routed directly to a stakeholder as part of the execution of a process instance. This architecture pattern turns a narrowly focused process that is concerned only with the entity data flowing through it into a contextually aware process capable of reacting automatically to changes in the organizational situation.

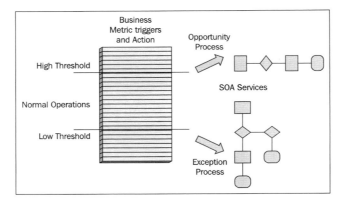

Context-aware decisions

Here, one can use business rules with organization-wide contextual BI information to drive business processes. This allows rules to take into account the wider state of the organization whilst making decisions on particular process instances.

The isolated execution of rules based only on the data within the current instance is not how decisions are normally made within an organization. Business context is as important within decisions as the data contained within the individual instance of an entity. Decisions on whether to loan money are not just based on the applicant's age or ability to pay, but also on wider business metrics, such as current availability to corporate credit, risk profiles, projected interest rates, and so on. Rules based on a narrow view of the instance alone are not enough to provide real organizational agility.

An addition to this pattern lies in the introduction of human workflow into an automated process. Stakeholders are required to interact with an automated process because they have some expert knowledge that cannot be automated as a business rule decision. This expert knowledge can be greatly enriched by the delivery of BI data to support the human decision. Therefore, at any human touch point within an automated process, contextual BI dashboards should be present in addition to information regarding the current task instance.

This architecture pattern allows business rules to operate on the insight gathered from the BI metric, allowing facts to be based on current organization and market context.

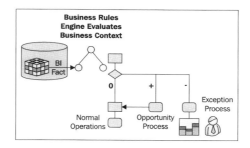

Technology requirements for combining BI and SOA

In order for technology to support these architectural patterns, your BI tool must support actions and must be able to deliver BI services to an external consumer. Your SOA toolset must be able to consume these BI services, embed BI data and dashboards into any human workflow elements, and be able to access these BI services as facts within a rule engine or decision service.

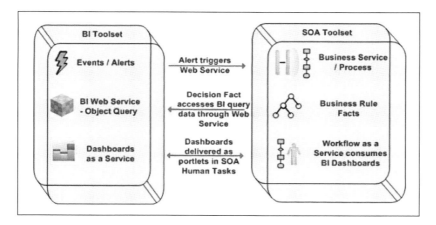

Building insight, actions, and context into processes

A few key principles must be adhered to when including decisions that are based on the wider business context for building processes that can react to immediate issues and/or opportunities:

- Process Design is an essential element, and must be modeled if you are going to use business context to dictate the path through a process, or to react to alerts that are raised within the execution of a process. Your modeling will take on extra dimensions. For instance, you may model two routes through a process, corresponding to high- or low-risk exposure.

- Business Activity Monitoring is a complementary event-driven approach to identifying and taking immediate actions based on real-time business occurrences. It is crucial in steering the business in the right direction. BAM and BI are necessary components in a complete solution for the provision of insight-driven business processes. BAM is intended to deal with the current state of operation, enabling a short lead time in reacting to issues or opportunities. BI takes a more analytical approach to guiding business processes or adding current enterprise context to individual instances of a business process. To draw a sailing auto-pilot analogy, BI helps determine the path/time to the next waypoint based on average speed, distance, and past trips. BAM, however, will refine the current path based on large waves, sudden wind changes, and any immediate obstacles.

- Understand and model the actions you want to take on the BI insight. A metric is much more effective if thresholds and actions are defined. When modeling BI metrics, it is important to think about the boundaries that will change the meaning of this metric (high, low, and so on) and then determine the business actions, normally defined as a process or rule change that should be performed to realign this metric. This adds key new dimensions to BI modeling.

- A consistent data model is required, and will be used by the business process, the business rules, and the BI/BAM elements. Combining BI and SOA means that you are sharing data between transactional and analytical systems. Common data models must be produced to support this. The data model will take account of metrics, thresholds, alerts, actions, and transactional data, with alerts and actions performing the role of mediator between the analytical world and the transactional world.

- Appreciate the different types of information services and source data from the most suitable type. Data for a business process can be provided via a number of different categories of data services, for instance, transactional data services where the data is current and reflective of the current process; business metrics which are normally analytical views of the data summarized through a relevant dimension; or complex decision services, where the data is the result of business rules. Choosing how to implement the data service at design time is key to the successful combination of BI and SOA. Decisions include determining which data sources are most relevant to be based on BI metrics, and which should be retrieved from transaction data services.

Business Scenario: Insightful processes for vehicle remarketing at Motability Operations

The Vehicle Remarketing initiative at Motability Operations offers an excellent illustration of the value of combining agile processes with business insight. The solution outlined showcases the potential of the technology and outlines the vision of what Motability Operations see possible as their vehicle remarketing solution evolves.

Motability Operations is a not-for-profit public company that runs the Motability Car Scheme. The largest fleet operator in the UK and the biggest supplier of used cars to the trade, Motability Operations is constantly challenged to create innovative, cost-effective, and efficient ways to market vehicles for sale as these vehicles reach the termination of their leases.

As vehicles approach the end of their leases, it is essential to push them to the most suitable sales channel, whether the channel is a direct sale website, a broker network, an auction site, or a consumer campaign. In a highly-competitive and saturated market, it is essential that the marketing channel and pricing model reflect customer needs and evolve as the market changes. Motability Operations must have insight into the performance of the vehicles on these channels and of the current market conditions in order to avoid any market saturation, whilst ensuring that the syndication and pricing of cars across the channels reflect buying behavior.

Syndication process and rule change based on business insight into sales channel and market performance

The business scenario looks to handle the market segmentation of cars by using BI and SOA to manage the mix of vehicle models and prices across the channels. The scenario uses insight provided by BI dashboards to trigger alerts that will automatically make changes to the business process, to rectify issues if the market is becoming saturated with a specific vehicle model. Extending this model, the business process is further enhanced to interrogate the BI objects containing information regarding the current performance of the sales channels, in order to better inform its decisions and flows. This extra market information gives insight into how busy the channels are, the current volume of a certain car model residing on the channel, or information into the sales performance on the channel.

The following screenshot illustrates an insight alert that is triggered on the dashboard because the volume of one of the channels is falling below a pre-determined threshold. The alert guides the user to an action that will rectify the problem, in this case a rule change to allocate cars of a slightly worse condition to this channel, in order to achieve an increase in volume.

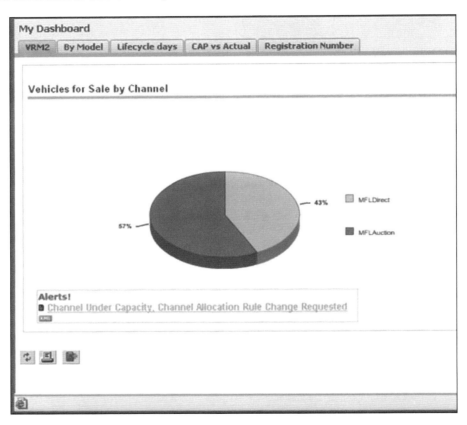

Authorization is required to enable such a change to business policy. A workflow task is raised to notify a user that a rule change has been suggested, based on channel insight. In order to allow the user to make the most intelligent and informed decision, relevant BI metrics are delivered as part of the task. These metrics give the user the wider context around sales performance, current pricing against market average, and consumer behavior on the channels. The user can then use the alert information with these additional measures to determine whether to accept the automatic change to the rules and process routing. This change cycle, incorporating business insight into the rule-changing process, will rectify the problem of low volumes on a given channel without affecting connected sales and profit metrics.

The next step is to automate the loop from business insight to business change. This can be done by automatically switching between different business process paths and business rule sets, as determined by the current market situation. If the business insight indicates that it is a quiet period for selling vehicles and that stock levels are high, an event could trigger an automated business change to switch to a low-sale-price business process and supporting rule set.

The business process for allocating cars to channels can utilize data sourced from a BI service to determine if the current market conditions and channel performance suit the particular instance of the vehicle the process is routing. This extra level of insight could result in the termination of the business process that was routing the car to that particular channel. In our business scenario, we might see an example in which there are too many cars of a specific model on an auction channel, saturating that channel and affecting sales volume. The business process would interrogate the BI metrics to determine the current channel stock situation and sales performance before syndicating the vehicles. Any vehicles determined to be unsuitable for the channel at this time would then be redistributed to the most relevant channel or queued until market conditions change.

Adding business rules to determine which channel is suitable based on the gathered insight enables automated redistribution, ensuring that the car is allocated to the channel that is most likely to produce the best price and quickest sale.

The previous figure shows the BPEL process that calls a BI service to gather current market performance. The process will have already determined the channels the vehicle is suitable for; this suitability is getting further enriched with the current situation of the channel. Using business rules based on this market insight enables the allocation process to take the channel situation into account when routing the car.

The next screenshot shows a dashboard view of the cars for sale on each channel. The same information is presented to **Business Process Execution Language** (BPEL) as channel insight through a BI service. The data indicates an abundance of cars of a particular model (Vauxhall Astra), resulting in low sales performance.

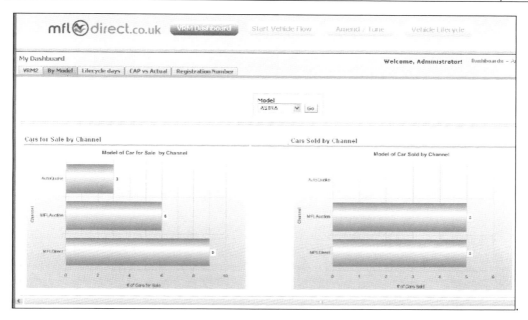

The following screenshot shows how any new Astras, which have been allocated to this channel, are disallowed.

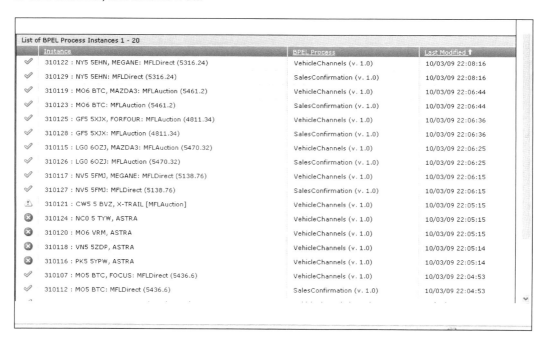

As a result, the vehicles flow down a different path of the BPEL process. A further reallocation process could be implemented, which would be invoked when the channel insight indicates that normal levels of the vehicle type have been restored. The vehicles could then be re-routed using BPEL and business rules.

Solution architecture for vehicle remarketing

The solution architecture for the business scenarios presented here is based on Oracle SOA Suite and **Oracle BI Enterprise Edition** (**OBIEE**), with the following components:

- BPEL Process Manager for the automation of business processes for marketing the vehicles and for the human workflow element to authorize syndication changes.

- Interactive BI dashboards for visibility into the current channel and market conditions, with a focus on the BI Delivers tool to produce alerts, delivering contextual dashboards to users, and initiating Web Services to start business processes and services to act on the information.

- Oracle Business Rules to provide agility by allowing immediate changes in the channel allocation policy that will take action on the alerts, without requiring an IT change cycle.

- Oracle ESB to provide mediation capability to switch between business processes and rule sets depending on the data provided by the dashboards.

- Web Services access into the Enterprise Information Model to make the dashboard information directly accessible by the business process, rules, and services.

In order to illustrate this architecture, let's walk through the solution components required for delivering the business scenario, describing the interaction between the components and any relevant technical implementation elements. The numerals below correspond to the numerals shown in the figure.

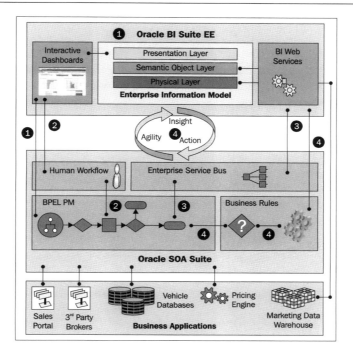

1. The business scenario starts with a guided alert within a dashboard. This alert informs the user that action must be taken to change an allocation rule, in order to restore a channel that has fallen below normal capacity.

2. When a threshold is exceeded, a "Channel Over Capacity" iBot (an alert based on user-specified conditions) is generated from the BI dashboard. This iBot uses a BI Delivers action to invoke the Channel Allocation Rule Change BPEL process.

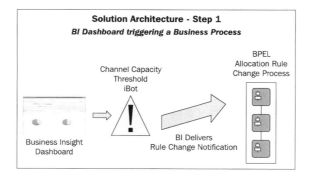

3. As part of the alert-driven change of rules to route more vehicles to a particular channel, a level of human authorization has been built into the solution. The BPEL flow that is invoked to deal with the Channel Allocation Rule Change will gather further information on the current channel performance, identify the most suitable modification to the rules, and then raise a task via the Human Task list Workspace for an analyst to authorize the rule change.

4. The task will include information relating to the rule change and will also present the analyst with contextual dashboards that provide all of the required information in one place. This eliminates the need to search for information through multiple screens or queries in business applications, process management engines, and BI tools.

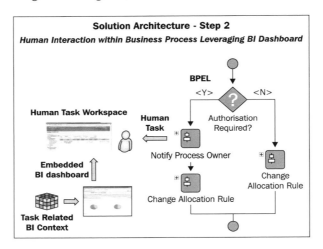

5. In order to allow a business process to access the BI Metrics that will allow current channel volumes to directly affect the process, BPEL accesses BI Web Services using Oracle ESB to mediate the request, and decouple the BPEL process from the BI Web Service call. This decoupling ensures that the Business Process in BPEL is shielded from any change in the structure of the BI objects.

The Channel Allocation BPEL flow will utilize a "Current Vehicle Saturation" Web Service to provide information from a Channel Summary BI object that shows the current sales performance for a channel before determining whether more vehicles of a specific type should be syndicated to that channel.

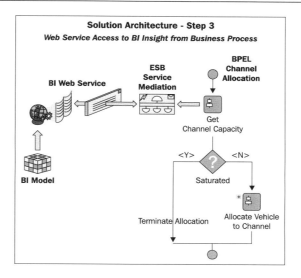

6. In order to fully automate and close the solution loop, a continuous alteration of rules can be implemented by using programmatic rule APIs to modify the structure, parameters, and boundary conditions of the business rules. This allows the solution to evolve, as dictated by business insight.

An alternative solution to this continuous approach to rule change is to build Java rule facts (data objects that are asserted when a rule is executed) within the business rule definitions that map directly to BI objects provided by the Web Services. Therefore, the rules will be based on facts, such as "low Channel Utilization", that will hand off the collection of the data which determines whether the channel is utilized by the BI objects.

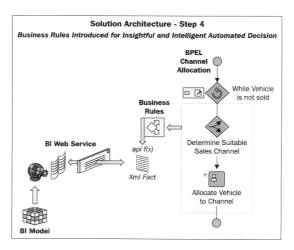

Solution benefits for Motability Operations

This article has described how the combination of BI and SOA allowed Motability Operations to address the challenge of selling each vehicle on the right channel at the right time for the right price. This goal was achieved through:

- Threshold breach alerts in dashboards, triggering the execution of business services to rectify issues like the market saturation of a vehicle type

- Business processes using BI insight to ensure the correct flow based on market and consumer behavior, such as the popularity of a certain vehicle on one channel

- Automated business rules that make decisions based on business insight, along with transactional data to enable channel allocation and pricing rules that take market performance into consideration

The architecture of this solution provides the ability to react to market changes and ensure that decisions on where to market vehicles are based not only on the vehicle details but also on the insight gathered from channel performance. This provides a wider market context in which to make vehicle routing decisions, and also allows closer alignment with how the business wants to operate.

When other factors, such as cost of the sale of the cars for each channel, or the cost of transferring cars, are taken into account and built into the solution, a comprehensive insight-driven allocation process that can implement an optimal and cost-saving business strategy for marketing the vehicles is produced.

Summary

The case study presented here illustrates the power of combining SOA with insight from BI. It also illustrates how your BI dashboards can be greatly enhanced through actions that will invoke services and processes. In such a solution there are a number of proven business and implementation patterns that will help with architecting the solution.

If agility is required within processes, it is the combination of SOA, process automation, business intelligence, and business rules that will provide the solution. This is a very compelling story to take to any business architect who wants to get the most out his/her processes and support any impending business change.

8

Building Enterprise 2.0 Applications

by Nam Doan-Huy, Yihong Xu, Narshimha Rao Kondapaka, and Melody Wood

In today's hypercompetitive global economy, agility in response to change is more important than ever. Information and the interaction around it have become key assets of most enterprises, and making good decisions in continuously shrinking cycle times is a defining operational characteristic of a successful company. This market imperative to access the right information, and deliver it to the right people at the right time, has led to an increased interest in building social enterprise capabilities—and the social web is central to that quest.

As businesses adopt these social collaboration tools within the enterprise to foster collaboration and increase the productivity of their employees, they also find that such tools are invaluable for achieving operational excellence. Enterprise 2.0 can play a vital role in allowing customers access to the organization's systems and processes. This level of ongoing collaboration with customers reduces the number of times that customers have to contact customer support, resulting in cost savings for the company and increased customer satisfaction.

How do you go about building an Enterprise 2.0 application? It's important to understand that it is not just building a Web 2.0 application. According to management consultants McKinsey & Company, Web 2.0 projects often are seen as grassroots experiments, and leaders sometimes believe the technologies will be adopted without management intervention—a "build it and they will come" philosophy.

Enterprise 2.0 applications, in contrast, serve business objectives and have support from internal (IT, business) and external (customers, partners) stakeholders. An Enterprise 2.0 technology strategy should combine the different aspects of Web 2.0 capabilities into a secure and comprehensive platform where business conversations and tasks are executed in the context of business goals. It should promote and enable rich user experiences and expose enterprise content in the most secure fashion. An Enterprise 2.0 application combines the capabilities of content management, security, search, and Web 2.0. It gathers information from ERP applications, CRM systems, and other backend enterprise applications and delivers this information in a form that is context based, secure, and easy to find.

In this chapter, we will examine the key building blocks of Enterprise 2.0 architectures and then outline important integration considerations for building an Enterprise 2.0 application. We will also look at how Wind River, a world leader in embedded and mobile software, leveraged Oracle's Enterprise 2.0 platform to revamp its online customer support portal.

Building blocks of Enterprise 2.0

Enterprise 2.0 is an integrative business strategy that combines multiple disciplines, technologies, and experiences. The fundamental capabilities of any rich Enterprise 2.0 strategy requires the combination of content management, a Web 2.0 framework, security, and integration with enterprise applications.

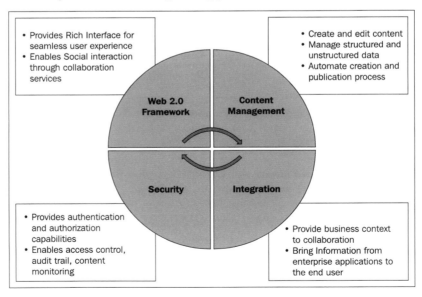

The following are the building blocks of Enterprise 2.0:

- **Content Management**: Organizations inadvertently deal with structured and unstructured data. Structured data can include documents, files, and videos, and is generated primarily from within the company. Unstructured data is generated mostly from customer interactions and could include blog postings, Wiki entries, and chat scripts. The content management platform provides a single and consistent infrastructure for managing, publishing, and delivering the data in a uniform fashion.

- **Integration**: Enterprise 2.0 brings information from ERP applications, CRM systems, and other backend enterprise applications together and presents it to the end user in a secure and contextual fashion. Users collaborate on information that is either coming out of, or going into, an enterprise application. This requires integration between enterprise applications orchestrating data and business flow, merging this data with the content management layer, and presenting it to the end user in a Web 2.0 frontend.

- **Security**: Enterprise 2.0 systems should be built with business in mind, with security as the highest priority. Exposing and personalizing content poses very specific security challenges, especially given the highly accessible and highly interactive nature of Enterprise 2.0 solutions. Who can publish and edit content? What happens to content over time? What user role-based restrictions should be placed on content? Enterprise 2.0 should be safe, secure, auditable, and controllable. The Security layer provides authentication, authorization, personalized delivery of content based on user roles and identities, a complete audit trail over the lifecycle of the content, and content publishing/monitoring controls.

- **Web 2.0 Framework**: While the content management platform addresses how content is created and managed, the Web 2.0 framework provides the collaborative platform to enable rich interaction through the ability to expose enterprise data in a highly collaborative manner. Due to the social nature of Web 2.0 platforms, it's important that this collaborative presentation layer is not only user friendly and easy to navigate, but that this single presentation layer is multi-channel accessible (by PCs, mobile devices, PDA, and other devices). Most importantly, the Web 2.0 framework enables conversational participation with users and systems through services like instant messaging, voice interaction, wikis, blogs, communities, tagging, user ratings, and personalization.

Enterprise 2.0 integration

With many technology tiers comprising several different products, it is important that these layers interact without any friction. Building Enterprise 2.0 frameworks in accordance with industry standards (mentioned below, such as JSR-170, JSR 168, BPEL, WSRP) helps to ensure interoperability with minimal code changes required. A standards-compliant platform also ensures flexible design architecture, allowing companies to scale their Enterprise 2.0 environments and easily fold in new features on an as-needed basis. Let's examine key integration considerations while building an Enterprise 2.0 application.

Integrating content management with the Web 2.0 layer

What's the best way to surface content from the content management layer in a rich UI? Is it possible to develop a flexible Enterprise 2.0 architecture that is agnostic of the portal or underlying content management framework? Fortunately, standards can play a significant role in reducing the pain of integration. Content management systems supporting the JCR or JSR-170 standards provide architectural flexibility. JSR-170-compliant content management systems can be accessed through a standardized API that can be used for connecting to any content repository. This removes the dependency of the Web 2.0 layer on the underlying content management platform. The Web 2.0 layer in turn can connect to several different content repositories without relying on hard-coded integrations.

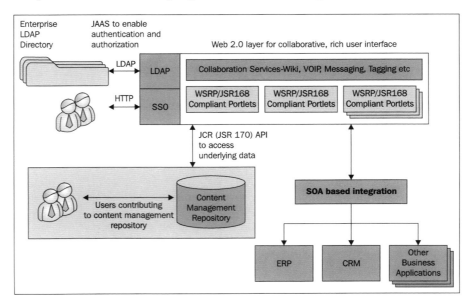

Similarly, JSR 168 (and its successor, JSR 286) and WSRP can provide interoperability between different portal vendors. With JSR 168 and WSRP, portlets are transformed into independent business objects that can be shared across different Enterprise 2.0 applications, thus promoting reuse.

Enabling authentication for the content management and Web 2.0 layers

Both the Web 2.0 and content management layers need to control access based on user profiles. Hence, configuration of the Web 2.0 and content management layers requires the use of Single sign-on for authentication and an LDAP provider as the identity store. To go beyond the limitations of J2EE security and to enable applications to authenticate users and enforce authorization, the most important standard is the **Java Authentication and Authorization Service** (**JAAS**), a standard security **Application Programming Interface** (**API**) that was added to the Java language through the Java Community Process.

Integrating the Web 2.0 layer with Enterprise applications using SOA

SOA plays an instrumental role in orchestrating business processes using **Business Process Execution Language** (**BPEL**). BPEL automates Web Services-based integration between different backend applications and humans. Integration between the Web 2.0 and SOA layers is bidirectional. Users from the Web 2.0 layer can kick-off or advance key business processes by calling BPEL processes directly. SOA, in turn, can deliver contextual enterprise data to the Web 2.0 layer.

Having outlined the basic architectural principles to augment an ECM solution with Web 2.0 capabilities, let us now examine the real-life application of these design principles in Wind River Systems' online customer support website.

Wind River's Enterprise 2.0 approach to online customer support

Wind River, the leader in the **Device Software Optimization** (**DSO**) market, wanted to fundamentally simplify information exchange and collaboration across its network of more than 30,000 employees and customers who used their **Online Support system** (**OLS**).

The company's original OLS was designed to support employees, customers, and partners on a unified development and delivery platform. The initial OLS goal was to provide a platform where customers and partners could get self-service access to personalized support data, log service requests, and find information on product defects and patches. That same platform was to allow employees (from Support, Product Management, Technical Publications, Engineering, and other departments) to contribute to the content collaboratively, and also to allow that content to be shared with customers. Unfortunately, that OLS system failed to meet those needs. It lacked the functionality as well as the infrastructure to display content that was targeted towards specific users.

The OLS infrastructure was based on various PHP/Perl-based CGI applications that delivered content from a variety of systems, including Oracle E-Business Suite and file-based and database systems. All support content (including support manuals, technical tips, FAQs, and how-to guides) was not centrally managed. The publishing process was completely manual and required a high level of coordination between Engineering, Product Management, and OLS staff. The lack of a centralized repository and the inability to dynamically update the documents created a maintenance nightmare for Wind River's support organization. Maintaining data integrity and minimizing the time to get new information to the customer was a major issue.

Another major complaint from customers was that they found it very difficult to find OLS content that was relevant to the products that they had purchased from Wind River. In order to address this issue, Wind River's vision was to personalize OLS content for each of its customers by showing them OLS content that was relevant to the products that they had purchased.

However, there was no infrastructure in place to link product and support content with the products that each customer had purchased from Wind River. This made it difficult to associate a customer's product install base with the content that the customer was seeing. This lack of centralized content and integration with enterprise systems had an adverse impact on customer experience. Customers were on their own to search or navigate Wind River's original OLS website in order to locate support data they might need. OLS also didn't provide the collaborative infrastructure that would allow customers and Wind River's support staff to interact in real time to quickly resolve customer issues.

Wind River took an Enterprise 2.0 approach to solve this challenge. It decided to centralize support content in a content repository and utilize a Web 2.0 interface to deliver targeted content from the content repository as well as other enterprise systems. How was this accomplished? Let's review the architecture.

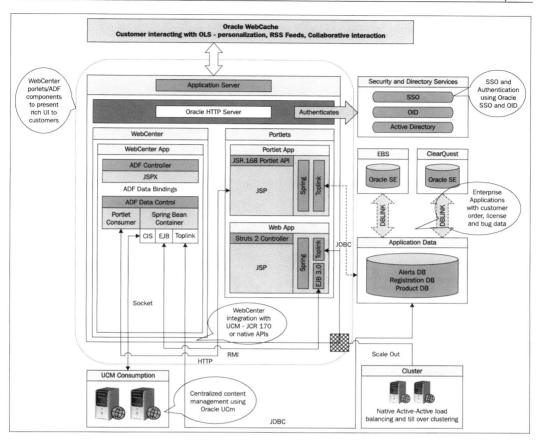

Content management

To centrally manage Wind River's product-related documents, patches, demos, digital assets, image files, and business process needs, the company chose **Oracle Universal Content Management** (**UCM**). UCM helps Wind River manage 3,000 to 5,000 physical files and about 78,000 digital files on the online support portal.

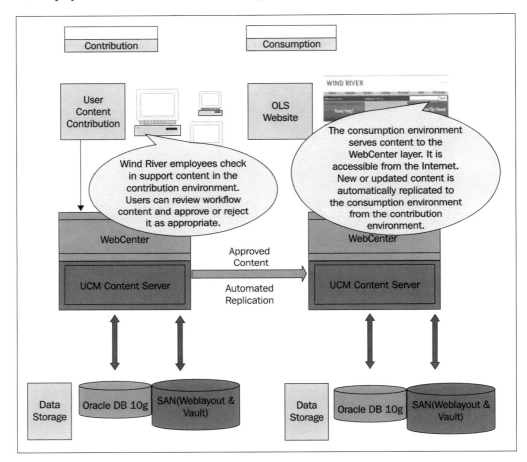

In addition to laying the foundation for a centralized customer delivery platform, UCM also streamlines the content publishing process. UCM effectively moves the ownership of publishing OLS content (manuals, patches, demos, and so on) away from various IT and online support administrators and directly to the content authors (Product Management, Engineering, Technical Publications, and so on) by creating an internal approval and publishing framework. This, in turn, reduces content processing inefficiencies and improves overall data integrity during the content contribution process.

Web 2.0

The OLS frontend was implemented using Oracle WebCenter. WebCenter has unique capabilities to build Enterprise 2.0 collaborative and social applications that seamlessly combine search, publishing, and knowledge management. WebCenter is based on technologies such as J2EE, **JavaServer Faces (JSF)**, and the **Oracle Application Development Framework (ADF)**. A combination of ADF components and portlets were used to build frontend user interfaces. The decision to build these components as ADF components or portlets was based on the following guidelines:

- **Portlet**: A portlet should be used if the component's functionality is based on only one system and it does not heavily interact with other components. An example of this type of component is the Proactive Alerts Subscription Form. This form takes input data from the user and stores it in the `Alerts` database. It does not interact with any other system and runs within itself. This type of component is an ideal candidate for a portlet. Also, if the component requires user-based customization, it should be built as a portlet.

- **ADF Component**: An ADF component should be used if the component interacts with other components on the page and its data can be driven from other components. While portlets are capable of intercommunication, ADF is the ideal choice if the interacting components are based on the same system.

The following screenshot depicts how the OLS home page, built using WebCenter, looks:

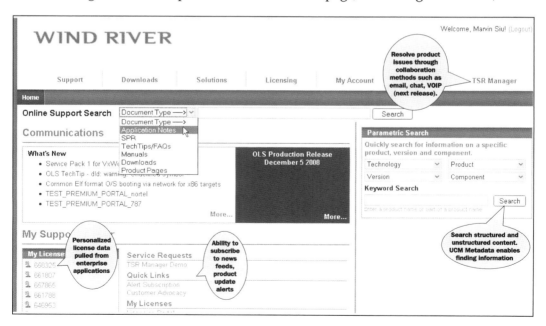

Our OLS frontend, built using WebCenter, makes it possible for customers to personalize their online support experience by subscribing to e-mail and content alerts in order to get the information they want.

Additionally, by planning to add further Web 2.0 features, such as discussion threads and chat capabilities to the site, Wind River aims to create a community of users that can provide each other with tips, best practices, and ideas for innovation in order to maximize their investment in Wind River technology.

Although Wind River had the option to use JCR-based integration with Oracle Universal Content Management, the company chose to integrate WebCenter with the UCM layer using **Content Integration Suite** (**CIS**). In addition to leveraging standard APIs, CIS offers caching and clustering features to boost performance. With CIS, a file system containing content can be mounted locally to the machine running the WebCenter server, making it local to WebCenter. This provides an additional performance boost, as a portal request does not need to go over the wire to search and fetch content. This is where the push-based content integration approach, which is extremely critical for features like RSS feeds, comes into play.

Security

There are different types of OLS users, and the security infrastructure needed to support these different types is identified as follows:

- **Public**: Public users should only be able to view and download product manuals.

- **Portal User**: Users who registered with OLS with no Wind River license (that is, they do not own any Wind River products) should only be able to update and add licenses to their profiles. They do not have access to OLS content.

- **Basic**: Users who registered with a valid license but who have no active Wind River product support. These users own Wind River products but have either allowed their product support to lapse or did not purchase product support. These users can access OLS but are restricted to viewing only basic content such as Tech Tips, Application Notes, and Manuals.

- **Maintenance**: Users who registered with a valid license that has active product support. These users own Wind River products and also have an active support service contract with Wind River. These users should be able to view all content in OLS except content restricted to Premium users.

- **Premium**: Maintenance users attached to a Premium Support account should be able to view all OLS content as well as premium content specific to their Premium Support account.

- • **Employee**: Employees should be able to view all OLS content, including premium content. Employees should also be able to view content that is inaccessible to customers, for example, unpublished defects and all service requests logged by customers (customers should only be able to see their own service requests).

Based on the above requirements, the following security model was designed for WebCenter and UCM:

- • WebCenter security model
- • UCM security model

WebCenter security model

OID	Register	Update Profile	Main Page	My Products	Product Search	Manuals	App Notes	Downloads	Tech Tips	Defects
Public	X					X				
Portal User	X	X				X				
Basic	X	X	X	X	X	X	X			
Maintenance	X	X	X	X	X	X	X	X	X	X
Premium	X	X	X	X	X	X	X	X	X	X
Employee	X	X	X	X	X	X	X	X	X	X

UCM security model

UCM Account	Manual	Download	TechTips	App Notes	Notification	Quick Links
Guest	X					
Basic	X			X	X	X
Maintenance	X	X	X	X	X	X
Premium_x	X	X	X	X	X	X
Employee	X	X	X	X	X	X

Premium_x in the UCM security model represents a UCM account. While *Premium_x* users are part of the Maintenance group, they may also have content that requires additional filtering. UCM accounts are used for this purpose. For example, downloads are accessible by all users in the OID Maintenance group. However, access to a particular downloadable document that is specific to the Premium Support account of *CompanyX* must be accessible only by those users in the Maintenance group who are also part of the OID group *Premium_CompanyX*. In order to accomplish this, the document in question is attached to the account *Premium_CompanyX*.

Additionally, metadata fields can also be used for security purposes. For example, Wind River uses a metadata field labeled `Internal`. If the value for this field is set to `true`, then the content is accessible only to employees. WebCenter, in establishing that contract with UCM, modifies the query if an employee is logged in, and passes the additional metadata field `internal = true` in the query.

Both WebCenter and the UCM layer leverage Oracle SSO/OID for authentication and authorization. UCM has an Identity Management plug-in that can be configured to retrieve user information from any LDAP-based directory. UCM also has configuration files to map LDAP group names to UCM Security Groups as well as UCM accounts.

For OLS, rather than using SSO for UCM, the UCM native authentication scheme was used. This is because UCM is not open to public users or all employees—only certain employees and content contributors can log in and modify content. However, UCM still authenticates against OID.

WebCenter is also configured to retrieve user information (roles and so on) from OID. However, SSO is configured to allow users to log in through SSO instead of the native authentication scheme. This is done by configuring SSO on the application server and identifying the application as SSO enabled. The page-level security is then enabled using J2EE security through `web.xml`.

The following steps occur when a user logs into OLS:

1. When a user navigates to an OLS portal page, the J2EE security configuration of OLS checks to see if the page is secured. This is done by examining the path of the page against the security constraint defined on the different paths of the application.

2. If the page is secured, the request is forwarded to the OID login module. If the page is not secured, then the request is forwarded to the page and no authentication is required.

3. The OID login module validates the user session. If the user is already authenticated, the login module forwards the request to the target page. Otherwise, the login module forwards the request to the SSO login page for authentication.

4. The user enters his/her credentials into the SSO login page, and they are validated against OID. Once the credentials have been validated, the user is forwarded to the login module.

5. The login module populates the user's OID profile from its cache. If the user is logging in for the first time, the profile is populated into cache from OID.

6. The user is then directed back to the original secured page that the user was trying to access. At this point, the J2EE security validates if the user's role is allowed access to the page.

7. If the user has access to the page (by virtue of being in the correct OID group), the request is forwarded to the page. Otherwise, an "Access Denied" page is displayed.

8. The target page utilizes UCM CIS queries to retrieve UCM data required by the target page. The user context (username) is also passed to CIS.

9. UCM loads the user profile from cache or OID based on the user context. Using the user's roles, security group, and account mappings, UCM filters the content retrieved by the CIS queries, and only returns documents that the user is allowed to view.

10. WebCenter renders the page based on the data returned by the CIS queries. As the data returned by CIS queries are user-context sensitive, each page will be rendered differently for different groups of users.

11. Portlets are rendered based on access control. WebCenter also provides the ability to hide or show any WebCenter components based on the user role. The J2EE user profile has a list of all the roles assigned to the user. All of the WebCenter components have a property called `rendered`. This property can be dynamically set to `true` or `false` based on any condition. The WebCenter component/portlet is rendered only if this property is set to `true`. Therefore, based on the list of roles, an evaluation can easily be performed to allow certain users to view certain components.

The following flowchart showcases how OLS Login, UCM, and WebCenter integrate:

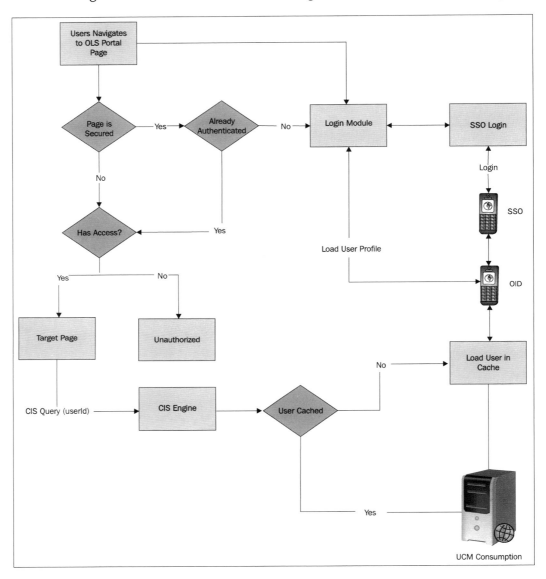

Based on the scenario shown in the previous figure, the queries for employees are also modified. If the user, who is currently logged in, is assigned the Employee role, all of the CIS queries are modified to add (xInternal 'TRUE') to get all the additional content items that should be visible to employees.

Integration

Wind River's vision was to enable customers to easily find support content that is relevant to them by matching the products each customer has purchased against content in UCM, and only displaying the matching content. This required OLS to integrate with **Oracle E-Business Suite** (**EBS**). It is this critical integration that provides OLS with the means by which it personalizes the content shown to each customer.

All Wind River customer information is stored in EBS, including each customer's product install base, license entitlement, and support contracts. Integrating with EBS enables OLS to match a customer's licensing and product install base, with relevant support content from UCM. In this way, OLS shows the customer support content that is relevant to what they have purchased, without the customer having to search or navigate OLS to find it.

Wind River used a combination of Oracle SOA Suite, TopLink, and database integration to deliver EBS information to UCM and WebCenter. The key to this integration was to map all content items in UCM to the product hierarchy in EBS. This allows us to query EBS to find out what products a customer owns, and then use that information to map those products to content items in UCM which are relevant to the customer.

UCM schema functionality is used to expose the product hierarchy in a tree view. A custom metadata field was also created on every content item type to hold the unique product identifiers that map each content item to a particular product. The tree view can then be associated with the metadata field to allow users to easily pick a product to which the content item will be attached. This enables OLS to map all UCM content items to products in EBS. For example, a VxWorks manual will be attached to the VxWorks product, and so on. The following screenshot illustrates the process:

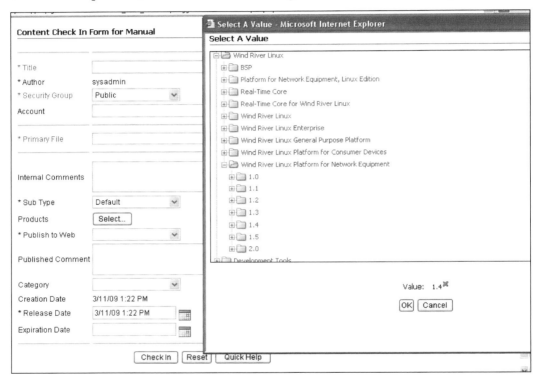

WebCenter integrates with EBS using TopLink to display personalized information via the **My Licenses** and **My Products** portlets. The **My Licenses** and **My Products** portlets play a key role in personalizing the content and navigation for each of Wind River's customers. The **My Licenses** portlet shows the customer all of the licenses associated with his or her OLS account. Clicking on a license number in **My Licenses** launches the **My Products** view, which provides the customer with a list of all of the products and versions licensed under that license number; all of this information comes from the integration with EBS, as shown in the following screenshot:

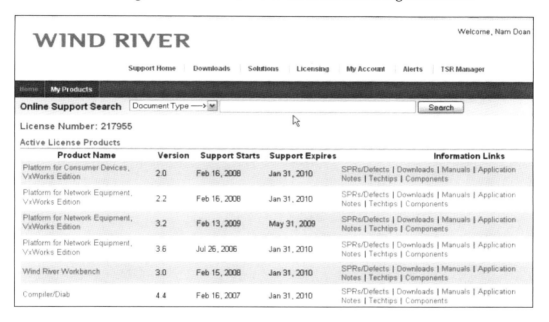

Next to each product and version, the customer will find links to all OLS content that is relevant to that particular product and version. For example, in the previous screenshot, consider the bottom product shown in the **My Products** view. By clicking on the **Manuals** link, the customer is able to easily find all of the manuals that have been mapped to **Compiler/Diab**, with **Version** as **4.4**. The resulting **Manuals** view is shown in the following screenshot:

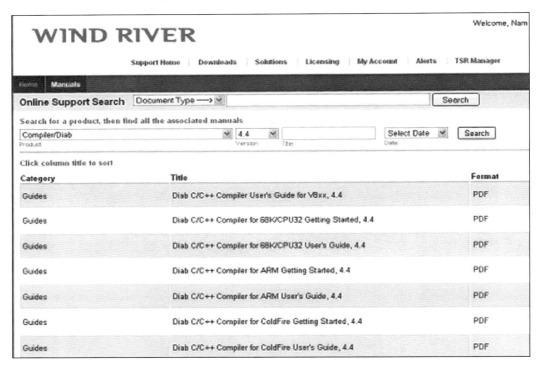

WebCenter generates the **Manuals** view with the content originating from UCM. WebCenter first makes a CIS call to UCM Consumption with the selected **Product** and **Version** as parameters of the CIS query. UCM then returns to WebCenter all content items of content type *Manual* that match the product and version provided. The data is then rendered by WebCenter in the **Manuals** view. The following figure illustrates the process flow:

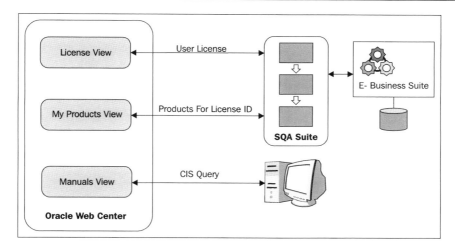

In this way, customers can go to the **My Products** view with one click (by clicking on the appropriate license number in **My Licenses**). OLS will then display all content that is relevant to the products and services the customer has purchased from Wind River. The customer does not need to search or navigate OLS to find that content. OLS shows it to them.

Summary

Wind River has achieved ROI on this project in three ways:

1. After collecting 14 months' worth of data following the launch of the new OLS, Wind River saw a 12% drop in the average number of total Service Requests logged per month, based on a month-to-month, year-on-year comparison, normalizing for the total number of Wind River customers under support.

2. All OLS content was previously manually maintained by the OLS team. For a major product release, it would take the OLS team weeks to manually publish the manuals, Application Notes, FAQs, and all other content associated with the product release to the OLS portal. UCM's self-service model has enabled Wind River's content authors, such as Technical Publications and Engineering, to easily review and publish their content for the product release without assistance from the OLS or IT teams. This has made the process seamlessly self-service and significantly reduced the time it takes for content to be published to OLS.

3. The personalized navigation has resulted in a 25% to 50% reduction in the number of clicks a customer needs to find the content they are looking for, depending on the content type. More importantly, instead of customers needing to navigate or search OLS to find content that is relevant to them, OLS now presents it to them. Customers no longer need to look for it. This has significantly contributed to reducing the number of clicks a customer needs to find relevant content, as well as playing a key role in increasing customer satisfaction.

As we can see with the Wind River OLS portal, Enterprise 2.0 is about bringing enterprise data to the end users in a highly secure and collaborative interface. Web 2.0, content management, and security play an important role in driving any Enterprise 2.0 strategy. A Web 2.0 layer can provide a single user interface to access content, process, systems, and people. Centralized content management enables a consistent contribution experience across multiple sites and applications. At the same time, content integrity minimizes risk and increases user adoption. Finally, security and privacy are at the core of Enterprise 2.0. SSO and role-based access, authentication, and authorization capabilities make Enterprise 2.0 safe, secure, auditable, and controllable.

Thanks to Melody Wood, Sanjay Kwatra, Sachin Agarwal, and Fahad Ansari for their valuable contributions.

For additional information visit the WebCenter Services Overview page at http://www.oracle.com/technology/products/webcenter/services.html#content.

9

Automating Enterprise Reporting with WebCenter, SOA, and Oracle Business Intelligence Publisher

by John Chung and Harish Gaur

The value of an enterprise reporting solution cannot be underestimated. To author, manage, and deliver all types of highly formatted documents against practically any data source is an extremely important functionality. Enterprises need such tools to generate thousands of reports for viewing and printing by employees, customers, partners, and others.

However, enterprise reporting can get complicated very easily. Not only does it have to generate **purchase orders** (**POs**) on the fly by acquiring data from multiple data sources, but it also has to personalize the look and feel of the report based on vendor country terms and conditions. The report has to adhere to the custom calendar schedule of the vendor—Vendor A in Canada should not get POs on July 1 (Canada Day), and Vendor B in India shouldn't get reports on August 15 (India's Independence Day). All reports should be generated only if internal business rules around PO limits and vendors' past performance are met. But that's not enough. Companies also need to automate the actual report compilation and generation process to ensure clear visibility into the reporting process. Otherwise, how can it be known whether a PO has been approved by the director of operations?

This business requirement is very typical in any business setting. Workflow and personalization are intrinsic to the reporting process, requiring the combination of a reporting platform, a process orchestration framework, and a collaborative portal. SOA offers an agile process orchestration framework, which can easily complement or enhance the enterprise reporting platform. Any reporting workflow could be automated by the SOA platform. SOA would enable humans to participate in the report approval process. Business rules could help generate reports on a conditional basis. With a process- and business rules-driven approach, visibility into the reporting process is much clearer. Similarly, a collaborative portal becomes a vehicle to deliver these reports in a personalized environment to the end users. Richly formatted reports could easily be delivered in a consistent manner, *helping to reinforce a particular brand*.

In this chapter, we will take a look at how to build an automated reporting platform with SOA, an enterprise reporting tool, and a portal. We will then walk through a real-life example. Arcturus, a leading real estate services company, built ClientConnect, a property management reporting solution using **Oracle Business Intelligence (BI)** Publisher, Oracle SOA Suite, and Oracle WebCenter.

Automated reporting platform architecture

Bringing SOA and a portal together in an enterprise reporting platform can allow users to develop flexible reporting solutions to meet a variety of business needs. SOA handles the data logic, and the reporting platform handles the layout and translation. This enables greater flexibility with report layouts, report maintenance, and optimization of the data extraction and document generation process.

Here are the six steps in the processing sequence, beginning with where the reporting process starts and ending at the point where the end user can see the personalized reports:

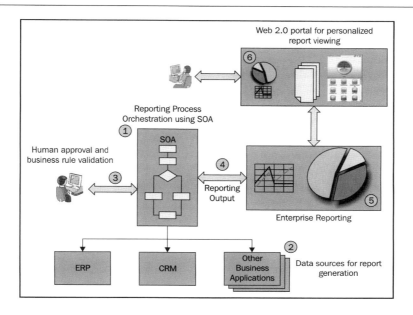

1. **Reporting process orchestration using SOA**: All process activities related to report compilation, such as data gathering, scheduling, personalization, rule validation, and human review, are modeled in a business process. This is traditionally accomplished using process orchestration engines like Oracle SOA Suite. The business process drives the entire report creation and delivery process. Any changes to how a report is created only impacts upon the SOA process. Using SOA to drive report generation also provides a definitive *immunity* from data source changes. If underlying data sources change at a later point of time, the SOA process could easily incorporate this change without affecting the end report. Similarly, if the business rule-driven report needs to be updated, this change would only be made in the rule sets. Another significant advantage comes from the ability to track processes, for example, how long it takes a user to review the report and where bad data in the report comes from. Such visibility can help identify deficiencies in the process.

2. **Data sources for report generation**: Once the report generation process is kicked off, it begins collecting data to be presented in a report to the end user. These data sources interact with the SOA process using Web Services. As discussed in the first step, this service-based approach offers certain flexibility to the overall process. Let's say report data is coming from SAP **Customer Relationship Management** (**CRM**) today. If the CRM system changes to Oracle Fusion CRM, it would not impact upon the report at all. Only the Web Service connecting the SOA process to Oracle CRM would need to be updated.

3. **Human approval and business rule validation**: Business rules play a very important role in the reporting process. Rules engines like Oracle Business Rules can help align the reporting process with business goals. For example, the SOA process will check the product inventory. Using business rules, the process will validate whether this inventory level is too high. If it is, then the SOA process would automatically generate a campaign letter to all customers. Rules can also be used to control the dissemination of reports to the end user. In the example, rules can determine if a campaign blast should be limited to customers who have purchased a similar product no later than a year before.

Similarly, human intervention can help put some controls into an otherwise automatic process. Oracle SOA Suite provides capabilities for humans to interact with the process. The Oracle BPEL Process Manager Human Workflow component manages the lifecycle of human tasks, including creation, assignment, expiration, deadlines, and notifications. In the example, sales managers could get a notification from the SOA human workflow asking them to review the campaign letter to be sent to all customers.

4. **Reporting output**: The SOA process can only handle business logic. Report formatting and translation are handled through the reporting platform. The handoff between SOA and the reporting engine is accomplished through XML. Reporting output generated after data collection, processing, and validation is handed off to the reporting engine in a specific XML format.

5. **Enterprise reporting**: The reporting engine takes processed XML data from the SOA process and creates the final report. It does so by applying the processed XML on its layout template (which can also be selected by the SOA process). For example, if you intend to produce the campaign report in PDF format, the layout template could be described in **Extensible Stylesheet Language-Formatting Objects** (**XSL-FO**), a markup language for XML document formatting that is most often used to generate PDFs.

Oracle BI Publisher is suited for enterprise reporting. Built on open standards, Oracle BI Publisher handles data in XML. It can generate reports in a wide range of industry standards such as PDF, HTML, **Rich Text Format** (**RTF**), Microsoft Excel, Microsoft PowerPoint, Flash, electronic data interchange, electronic fund transfer, and comma-separated values. Oracle BI Publisher also provides a Web Service interface to integrate with the SOA layer. These Oracle BI Publisher Web Services can be used to generate and schedule reports, manage reports and folders, and validate user report access.

6. **Web 2.0 portal for personalized report viewing**: The final report is delivered to the end user in a personalized portal platform. In addition to a consistent user experience, the portal platform provides the capability to embed key Web 2.0 features. This could also be the interface to interact with the SOA process via human workflow services. Oracle WebCenter Suite is an ideal platform to deliver a rich user experience by combining diverse content and allowing users to collaborate through social computing services. Oracle WebCenter can easily bring in human workflow data from SOA and display Oracle BI Publisher reports. This makes Oracle WebCenter a singular platform for user interaction during report creation and report viewing.

Now that we have seen critical components of the solution, let's see how Arcturus built ClientConnect, its property management reporting solution.

Property Management Reporting Solution at Arcturus

Arcturus is a real-estate services firm specializing in property and facilities management, asset management, leasing, and advisory services. They manage more than 600 properties (a mix of commercial, retail, and industrial). Each building exists as its own business entity, and on a monthly basis, Arcturus provides its clients (the landlords or asset managers) with a management report that includes an executive summary, financial statements, variance analysis on budget to actual, leasing (sales) information and forecasting, occupancy statistics and stacking plans, cash flow, and operational reports. Although the number of buildings amount to more than 600, the number of reports the company generates on a monthly basis is in the thousands.

However, the report generation process is highly complex (refer to the following figure). Three key groups are involved in delivering the reports—accounting, leasing, and property management. Data was pulled from several data sources including Oracle's **JD Edwards**, content servers, and databases. On a monthly basis, Arcturus closes off the period for the property, and each group is responsible for their sections.

The accountants compile the numbers, and then send them to the property managers (some back and forth communication generally happens missed: accruals, discrepancy of numbers, and so forth). Each time a change is made, the accountants will rerun the financial statement and e-mail it to the property manager. Upon approval of draft financials, the property manager manually rekeys the financial data in relevant fields within the management report template, and adds text comments and additional reports where required. The entire report is manually arranged in sections. Then it is combined into one PDF document (including the JD Edwards financials, which are PDFs; thus, they are converted to PDF twice) and e-mailed to the client or posted on ClientConnect, the Arcturus report repository.

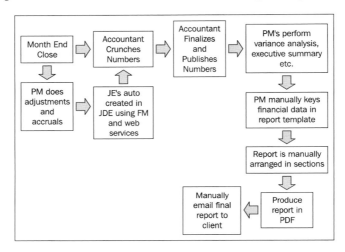

This manual process led to several issues. Most importantly, the delivery of reports required a lot of staff time due to inefficiencies in task resourcing and management. Disjointed collaboration between groups led to missed timelines and finger-pointing. There were several data inconsistencies and inaccuracies due to the manual rekeying of financial data into report template results. For example, the JD Edwards income statement data was manually keyed into the executive summary.

Arcturus decided to automate the entire process of report compilation and generation using Oracle Fusion Middleware.

ClientConnect solution

Arcturus chose Oracle Fusion Middleware to orchestrate and facilitate the monthly reporting process. *The main objective of the project was to automate the monthly reporting process and to deliver reports to the end users* in a rich collaborative environment.

As shown in the following figure, the solution consists of Oracle SOA Suite (Oracle BPEL Process Manager, Oracle Business Activity Monitoring, Oracle Business Rules, Oracle Human Workflow), Oracle WebCenter, and Oracle BI Publisher. As soon as data changes in the JD Edwards table, **Oracle Enterprise Service Bus** (**ESB**) picks up the changes and kicks off the BPEL process. The BPEL process orchestrates the entire reporting process. Oracle BI Publisher is the reporting engine that takes processed data from Oracle BPEL Process Manager and produces a highly formatted report. The Arcturus Portal, built on Oracle WebCenter technology, delivers the report to property managers. It also displays human task lists and business activity monitoring dashboards. Business activity monitoring dashboards (Phase 2) provide the operational visibility into the reporting process.

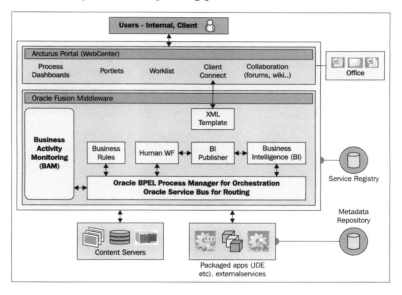

To understand how the solution is integrated, let's walk through a use case. In this scenario, property data and canned reports are captured from JD Edwards EnterpriseOne with Oracle ESB. Once captured, BPEL pushes this data through various approvers in the accounting and property management groups. Once approved, this data is passed on to Oracle BI Publisher for report generation. Oracle BI Publisher generates the property report on the fly. This report is then surfaced in Oracle WebCenter for end users. So, let's see what this process looks like.

1. The ESB captures reporting data from JD Edwards and kicks off the BPEL process.
2. The BPEL process starts the report compilation process.
3. BPEL invokes Oracle BI Publisher to generate reports.
4. Arcturus Portal delivers reports to property managers.

We will look at these steps in detail in the following sections.

Step 1: The ESB captures reporting data from JD Edwards and kicks off the BPEL process

The reporting process is started once a company's month is closed for both **accounts payable (AP)** and **accounts receivable (AR)** by a user within JD Edwards through the company master.

As the month closes, important property data is pushed from JD Edwards to the ESB. Various details about the specific property are published from JD Edwards. This includes business unit number, period, year, report type, general ledger account number, names, and balance for reconciliation. In addition, the following critical financial information about the property is obtained from JD Edwards:

- Income statement data
- Rent roll
- Lease expiration information
- Accounts receivable information
- Open POs (used to generate accrual tasks)

The ESB uses a database adapter to poll data from JD Edwards, as illustrated in the following figure. It reads the table that identifies whether AP/AR has been closed. As soon as records are found to be true, it will initiate the BPEL process.

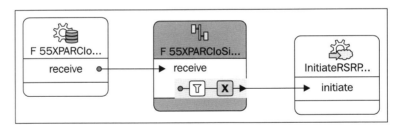

In this example, **F55XPARClo...** is a database adapter that connects to the JD Edwards database to poll the table and check if there is a need to initiate or run a BPEL process; that is, if AP/AR is closed, it will pick up that record and initiate or run a BPEL process. The middle *activity* then receives the data polled from the JD Edwards table and does the transformation, passing it to the input parameters of the BPEL process.

The following screenshot shows the transformation (mapping) from the database adapter to the SOAP input parameters. It maps the columns selected from the database to the input parameters of the BPEL process. For example, column `xamcu` of the database table is passed and mapped to the other side as `businessUnit`.

Step 2: BPEL process starts report compilation process

The BPEL process takes property data from the ESB and orchestrates the monthly reporting process through a series of human tasks. The process involves tasks where property data and canned JD Edwards reports are pushed to users for approval. This is accomplished through the human workflow capability of the Oracle BPEL Process Manager. Let's see what the BPEL process looks like and what role human workflows and business rules have in the process.

The following figure shows the parent BPEL process. Each step in the process represents a subprocess where most of the process orchestration is performed.

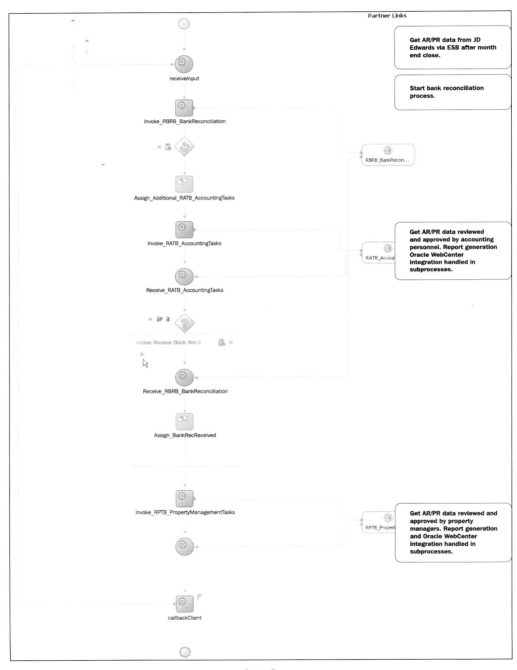

BPEL Human Workflow allows users to view tasks in an Oracle BPEL work list application (UI). Users can then view the data/reports online, select/add records (general ledger amounts) to be accrued/adjusted, and add commentary for the published report. The tasks must be completed in succession, where each task must be actioned by a user in order for the process to continue and result in the compilation of the final report. The BPEL process dynamically determines who the approvers are for a specific property report.

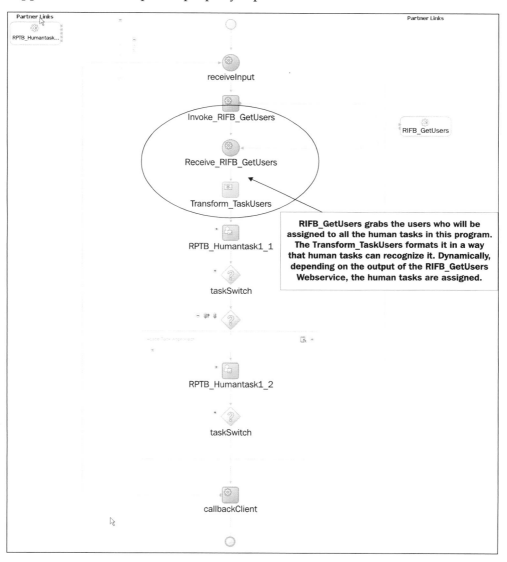

RIFB_GetUsers grabs the users who will be assigned to all the human tasks in this program. The Transform_TaskUsers formats it in a way that human tasks can recognize it. Dynamically, depending on the output of the RIFB_GetUsers Webservice, the human tasks are assigned.

When a human task is processed, the assigned user will receive an e-mail notification, which contains a direct link to the task page on the UI. Once users log in, they are directed to the specified task. In the sample task, as shown in the following screenshot, the user (general manager/director) is approving the property management report as submitted by the property manager. The user can view the draft PDF copy of the property management report embedded as a link at the bottom-right. The user has various options—approve (as is), add internal commentary regarding changes/edits and send back to originator, or reject the task entirely if the financials are incorrect and data changes are required.

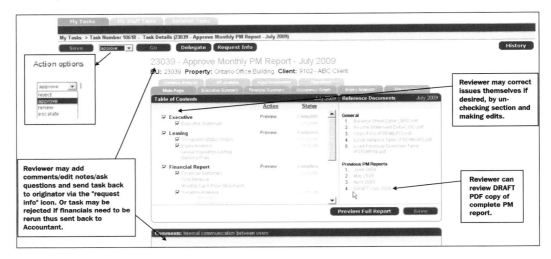

Business rules play an important role during this orchestration. The process primarily involves two groups, accounting (A) and property management (P), *where levels of approval might be required for tasks, that is, where P1 tasks require approval by P2, or A1 tasks require approval by A2.* Prior to each human task, BPEL reads the business rules to determine, based on the property, which user is to receive a task; or in the case of approvals, whether approval is required or not. This is achieved by populating the rules with JD Edwards category code numbers that represent a corresponding role—property manager (P1), director (P2), accountant (A1), and accounting manager (A2). The category code number refers to the category code number in the business unit *setup* within JD Edwards, which houses the address book number of the assigned user. Through all this, necessary user information is gathered so the task can be directed accordingly by business unit/property. A skip approval function is also used within the business rules via a unique variable.

Refer to the following four screenshots to visualize how a **variance threshold rule** has been created at the client level (#9071). This threshold checks whether the year-to-date actual versus the year-to-date budget variance is (> $1000.00 or < -$1000.00) AND (> 10% or < -10%). Both conditions must apply. The BPEL process can invoke this rule to see if threshold checks are met. In the rules editor, all threshold rules for different clients are set. In the following screenshot, we can see five threshold rules defined under the ruleset.

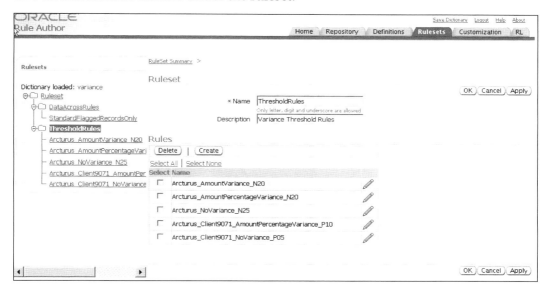

Now, we select ThresholdRules `Arcturus_Client9071_AmountPercentageVariance_P10`. Here, one can modify rule **Name** and **Priority**. Higher priority rules run before lower priority rules, within a ruleset. The default priority is medium (with the integer value `0`).

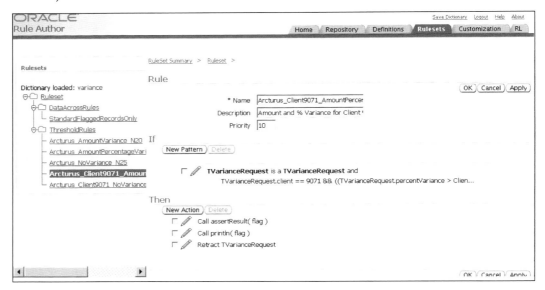

Once we set the priority, we will set the actual rule definition. In this case, threshold checks whether the year-to-date actual versus the year-to-date budget variance is (`> $1000.00` or `< -$1000.00`) AND (`> 10%` or `< -10%`). This is accomplished not by using absolute numbers, but with variables.

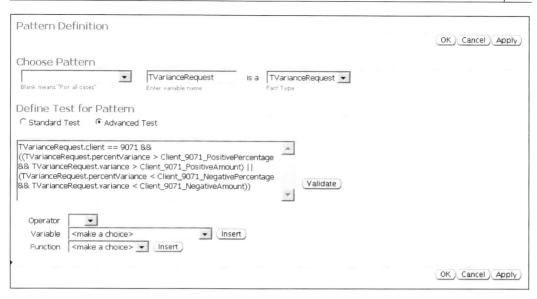

Variable values are manipulated here. You can use variable definitions to share information among several rules and functions. For example, variable `StandardPositiveAmount` could also be used by another rule. Using variable definitions can make programs modular and easier to maintain.

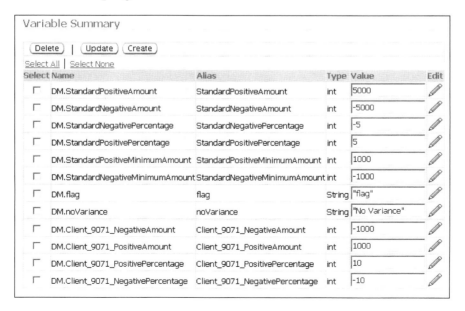

We just saw how the BPEL process with the help of human workflow and business rules drives the entire report compilation process. Throughout this process, property reports are generated for different approvers to review. Let's see how BPEL integrates with Oracle BI Publisher to generate reports.

Step 3: BPEL invokes Oracle BI Publisher to generate reports

As previously mentioned, Oracle BI Publisher offers most of its functionality through a Web Service API. Developers can use the Web Service API to generate and maintain reports. Calling the Oracle BI Publisher Web Service from Oracle BPEL Process Manager is very simple.

Although we could have called the Oracle BI Publisher Web Service directly from BPEL, we integrated Oracle BI Publisher with BPEL through its Java API component. This was done for two reasons:

- We enhanced the functionality of UI to view the report on the fly just by clicking a button.
- Our strategy is to only write the whole process to the database once it's done. All the data/information we need to create the report is in the payload.

The Java program connects to BPEL and accesses the payload, generates the XML data needed by the template, and uses the Oracle BI Publisher API to merge them. The program accesses the FOProcessor and RTFProcessor methods to handle the necessary transformation of the XML input to its corresponding PDF output.

- RTFProcessor converts an RTF template to XSL in preparation for input to the FOProcessor engine.
- The FOProcessor engine merges XSL and XML to produce any of the following output formats—Microsoft Excel (HTML), PDF, RTF, or HTML.

Using Oracle JDeveloper, this program is quickly converted into a Java Web Service. Once the Java Web Service is deployed, the URL for the deployed **Web Services Description Language (WSDL)** is used to link it to BPEL. The following sample code shows how the report accepts XML data from BPEL and calls Oracle BI Publisher APIs.

```
Import oracle.apps.xdo.XDOException;
import oracle.apps.xdo.common.pdf.util.PDFDocMerger;
import oracle.apps.xdo.template.FOProcessor;
import oracle.apps.xdo.template.RTFProcessor;

/* Obtains the instance of BPEL process running in a process domain.
This process instance has the needed XML to generate the report */
```

```
wfSvcClient = WorkflowServiceClientFactory.getWorkflowServiceClient(Wo
rkflowServiceClientFactory.SOAP_CLIENT);
ITaskQueryService querySvc = wfSvcClient.getTaskQueryService();

wfCtx = querySvc.authenticate("oc4jadmin", "abc123","myrealm",null);
ServerAuth auth = ServerAuthFactory.authenticate(securityCredentials,
null, props);
Server srv = new Server(auth);


Locator locator = new Locator(srv.getDomainStatus("prod").
getDomainId(), securityCredentials, props);


WhereCondition whereProcessId = new WhereCondition("process_id = ?");
whereProcessId.setString(1, "BankReconciliationProcess");


WhereCondition whereInstanceId = new WhereCondition("cikey = ?");
whereInstanceId.setLong(1, instanceId);

whereProcessId.append("and");
whereProcessId.append(whereInstanceId);
IInstanceHandle[] instances = locator.listInstances(whereInstanceId);

/* This section enables the application to parse the XML from BPEL */

DocumentBuilderFactory documentBuilderFactory =
DocumentBuilderFactory.newInstance();
DocumentBuilder documentBuilder = documentBuilderFactory.
newDocumentBuilder();
Document document = documentBuilder.newDocument();
Element payload = document.createElement("payload");
document.appendChild(payload);

/* Using BPEL Instance Handle, BPEL XML is parsed and readied for
processing by Oracle BI Publisher */

Element elementBankRec = (Element)instances[0].
getField("BankRecVariable");


Element elementAccountLevel = (Element)instances[0].getField("AccountL
evelVariable");
Element elementSignOffDates = (Element)instances[0].getField("SignOffD
atesVariable");
Element elementSigPaths = (Element)instances[0].
getField("SigPathsVariable");


payload.appendChild(elementBankRec);
payload.appendChild(elementAccountLevel);
```

```
payload.appendChild(elementSignOffDates);

/* Converts an RTF template created in Word to XSL in preparation for
input to the FO engine. Out1 is the output file */

FileOutputStream tempBankRecfos = new FileOutputStream(filename);

RTFProcessor rtfProcessor = new RTFProcessor("/home/oracle/file_
repository/reports/templates/bankrec.rtf");
rtfProcessor.setOutput(out1);
rtfProcessor.process();

/* FO engine merges XSL (template from RTFProcessr) and XML (from
BPEL) to produce PDF report. SetData sets XML Input and setTemplate
sets XSL Input */

FOProcessor processor = new FOProcessor();
ByteArrayInputStream arIs = new ByteArrayInputStream(
documentToString(payload).getBytes() );
processor.setData(arIs);
processor.setTemplate(new ByteArrayInputStream(out1.toByteArray()));
processor.setOutput(tempBankRecfos);
processor.setOutputFormat(FOProcessor.FORMAT_PDF);
processor.generate();
```

The following code shows what the BPEL XML, RTF template, and final report with populated BPEL data looks like. This data came from the human task payload, which was submitted by the user, and the amount displayed was encoded through the UI.

```
<?xml version="1.0" encoding="UTF-8" ?>
<task xmlns="http://xmlns.oracle.com/bpel/workflow/task">
  <title>23041 - Approve Bank Reconciliation - July 2010</title>
  <payload xmlns="http://xmlns.oracle.com/bpel/workflow/task">
    <EmailAddress xmlns="http://www.arcturusrealty.com/emailAddr">
      <userName>rsathiyana</userName>
      <email>rsathiyananthan@arcturusrealty.com</email>
    </EmailAddress>
    <Accountants xmlns="http://www.arcturusrealty.com/AccLevel">
      <Accounting1>Aida Cardenas</Accounting1>
      <Accounting2 />
    </Accountants>
    <SignOffDates xmlns="http://www.arcturusrealty.com/SignOffDates">
      <Date1>2010-08-03</Date1>
      <Date2 />
    </SignOffDates>
    <SignaturePaths xmlns="http://www.arcturusrealty.com/SigPaths">
      <PreparedBy>//home//oracle//file_repository//reports//images//
        signatures//cp_217267_ACARDENAS_Signature.jpg</PreparedBy>
```

```
    <ApprovedBy />
  </SignaturePaths>
  <balance_as_per_bank_statement
    xmlns="http://www.arcturusrealty.com/bankRec">
    48188.16</balance_as_per_bank_statement>
  <less_outstanding_items_as_per_reconciliations_report
    xmlns="http://www.arcturusrealty.com/bankRec">
    675.42</less_outstanding_items_as_per_reconciliations_report>
  <addCollection xmlns="http://www.arcturusrealty.com/bankRec" />
  <lessCollection xmlns="http://www.arcturusrealty.com/bankRec" />
  <addTotal xmlns="http://www.arcturusrealty.com/bankRec" />
  <lessTotal xmlns="http://www.arcturusrealty.com/bankRec" />
  <reconciliation_total
    xmlns="http://www.arcturusrealty.com/bankRec">
    48863.58</reconciliation_total>
  <balance_per_general_ledger
    xmlns="http://www.arcturusrealty.com/bankRec">
    48863.58</balance_per_general_ledger>
  <reportParameters
    xmlns="http://www.arcturusrealty.com/ReportParameters">
    <BusinessUnit>23041</BusinessUnit>
    <Property>360 Laurier Avenue West</Property>
    <Month>July</Month>
    <Year>2010</Year>
    <Client>9102-Slate Properties Inc.</Client>
    <Mode>Review</Mode>
    <ManagementOffice />
    <Period>7</Period>
    <FiscalYear>10</FiscalYear>
    <taskExpiration>P1D</taskExpiration>
    <Type>M</Type>
  </reportParameters>
</payload>
<taskDefinitionURI>http://soaweb1.arcturus.local:7777/orabpel/
  prod/BankReconciliationProcess/3.0/HumanTask2/HumanTask2.task
</taskDefinitionURI>
<ownerUser>bpeladmin</ownerUser>
<priority>3</priority>
<identityContext>myrealm</identityContext>
<userComment>
  <comment>Ratha: July-2010 Bank reconciliation is completed for
    360 Laurier</comment>
  <updatedBy>
    <id>acardenas</id>
  </updatedBy>
  <updatedDate>2010-08-03T11:47:36-04:00</updatedDate>
```

```xml
</userComment>
<userComment>
  <comment>Approved</comment>
  <updatedBy>
    <id>rsathiyana</id>
  </updatedBy>
  <updatedDate>2010-08-03T11:50:28-04:00</updatedDate>
  <action>ROUTED</action>
</userComment>
<attachment>
  <mimeType>application/pdf</mimeType>
  <name>July 2010 Bank Statement & outstanding chq List 360
    Laurier.pdf</name>
  <updatedBy>acardenas</updatedBy>
  <taskId>32687d765b75fb16:3b24ea99:128ee025f4d:2840</taskId>
  <version>3</version>
</attachment>
<processInfo>
  <domainId>prod</domainId>
  <instanceId>217267</instanceId>
  <processId>BankReconciliationProcess</processId>
  <processName>BankReconciliationProcess</processName>
  <processType>BPEL</processType>
  <processVersion>3.0</processVersion>
</processInfo>
<systemAttributes>
  <approvalDuration>696660408</approvalDuration>
  <assignedDate>2010-07-26T10:19:34-04:00</assignedDate>
  <assigneeUsers>
    <id>rsathiyana</id>
    <displayName />
  </assigneeUsers>
  <createdDate>2010-07-26T10:19:34-04:00</createdDate>
  <digitalSignatureRequired>false</digitalSignatureRequired>
  <endDate>2010-08-03T11:50:34.408-04:00</endDate>
  <expirationDate>2010-08-04T11:48:19-04:00</expirationDate>
  <hasSubTasks>false</hasSubTasks>
  <inShortHistory>true</inShortHistory>
  <isGroup>false</isGroup>
  <numberOfTimesModified>10</numberOfTimesModified>
  <outcome>APPROVE</outcome>
  <passwordRequiredOnUpdate>false</passwordRequiredOnUpdate>
  <pushbackSequence>-1-6-7-10</pushbackSequence>
  <secureNotifications>true</secureNotifications>
```

```
    <state>COMPLETED</state>
    <taskId>32687d765b75fb16:3b24ea99:128ee025f4d:2840</taskId>
    <taskNumber>10774</taskNumber>
    <updatedBy>
      <id>rsathiyana</id>
    </updatedBy>
    <updatedDate>2010-08-03T11:50:34.409-04:00</updatedDate>
    <version>10</version>
    <versionReason>TASK_VERSION_REASON_COMPLETED</versionReason>
    <taskDefinitionId>prod_BankReconciliationProcess_3.0_HumanTask2
    </taskDefinitionId>
    <taskDefinitionName>HumanTask2</taskDefinitionName>
  </systemAttributes>
  <systemMessageAttributes />
  <callback />
</task>
```

The Oracle BI Publisher template in the following screenshot receives the XML data through the Oracle BI Publisher API, and transforms the output to PDF format.

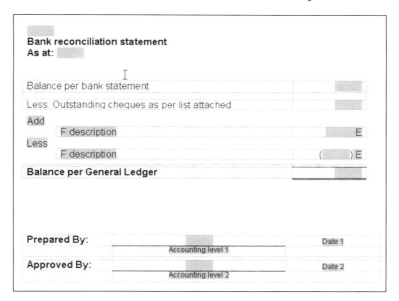

In the following screenshot you will see the generated PDF output from the combined XML data/payload submitted by the user and the Oracle BI Publisher template. The signature is also automatically attached to the template as soon as users approve the task assigned to them.

arcturus

425 Bloor St. East
Bank reconciliation statement
As at: February 28, 2010

Balance per bank statement	$150,857.08
Less: Outstanding cheques as per list attached	(11,769.86)
Less:	
Arcturus LP (Amex)	1,132.28
Bank error Feb 16, 2010	4,486.23
Balance per General Ledger	**$133,468.71**

Prepared By: Aida Cardenas 2010-03-01

Approved By:

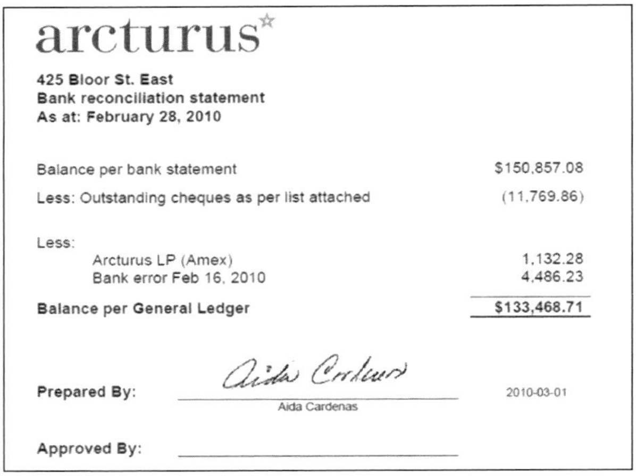

We see how the Oracle BI Publisher API is wrapped as a Java Web Service and called from BPEL. This Java Web Service takes XML data from BPEL and merges it with the report template to create the final report. Now, let's see how end users see this report in the Arcturus Portal.

Step 4: Arcturus Portal delivers reports to property managers

The Arcturus Portal, built using Oracle WebCenter, is a unified platform to view reports, approve tasks, and get connected with peers. Two important facets of this portal are:

- How Oracle BI Publisher reports are integrated into the portal
- How human tasks are integrated into the portal

BPEL will send the generated final output report to a structured folder on the Arcturus Portal Server. From there, users are able to access the complete report through the Oracle WebCenter Document Library component. The Oracle WebCenter application uses an **Application Development Framework** (**ADF**), `fileDownloadActionListener`, in conjunction with a backing bean to download the PDFs.

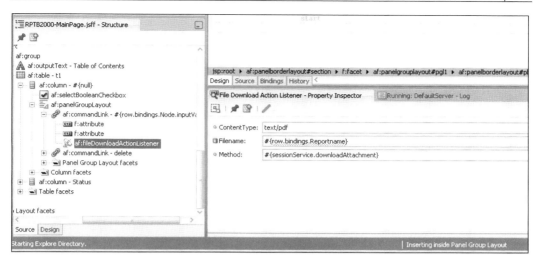

Human task lists are also integrated with the Arcturus Portal. Users log in to the **Task List WebCenter** application and view their assigned Human Tasks. **Human Tasks** are the frontend human interaction web pages provided by a connection to the SOA-BPEL application. The ADF `ViewController` project is used to display a list of tasks and links to SOA Human Tasks along with Oracle WebCenter components and features on the Web. The following screenshots show how property managers use WebCenter to review and download reports.

In the next screenshot, you can see how Oracle BPEL Worklist UI has been integrated with Oracle WebCenter. A user is able to review and approve various tasks right from the WebCenter dashboard.

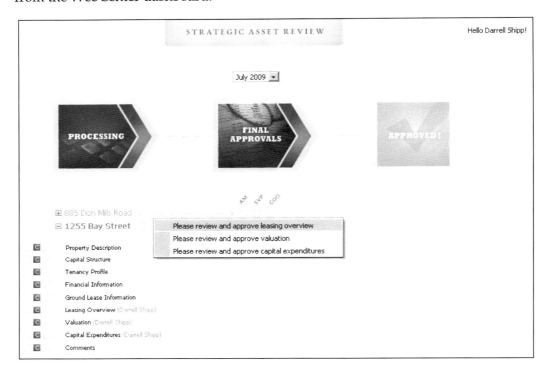

Users can also download reports directly from WebCenter interface. This highlights the integration between WebCenter and BI Publisher.

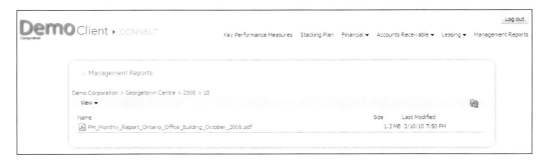

In the following screenshot, we see what the final report looks like. BI Publisher reports are displayed alongside ADF portlets.

As you can see, this solution (combining Oracle SOA Suite, Oracle WebCenter, and Oracle BI Publisher) automated the entire property management reporting process for Arcturus. The result was a more transparent process enabling cohesive collaboration between the accounting and property management groups. One of the biggest advantages Arcturus sees from this solution is the ability to track tasks within processes. This provides management with the ability to identify potential issues and solutions to ensure reports are delivered to the client on time, and proactively mitigate risk where timelines might be affected.

Data *auto population* resulted in a 50 percent reduction in the time and effort (per property report depending on size of report) required by property managers to compile and transpose data into a report. The total report cycle per report was reduced by 40 percent, and Arcturus estimated ROI in less than two months. Arcturus is looking to implement a similar solution in other key areas, such as contract management, new property transition/property disposition, and employee hire/termination.

Summary

Enterprise reporting can greatly benefit from SOA and portal platforms to create an agile, personalized reporting platform. SOA can complement the reporting tool to manage crucial human interventions and align reports with constantly changing business goals. The portal platform provides a unified interface to deliver reports in a consistent and personalized environment. With the existence of standards like BPEL, Web Services, WSRP, and XML, it is simpler than ever to integrate all these pieces in a seamless manner. Organizations can greatly benefit from reduced manual processing and improved visibility into the entire reporting process.

10

A Role-based Approach to Automated Provisioning and a Personalized Portal

by Rex Thexton, Nishidhdha Shah, and Harish Gaur

Customers, partners, and employees all need access to enterprise data. But as IT enterprises grow more complex with new systems, interfaces, and applications, it becomes increasingly challenging to control and monitor who can access what IT resources.

Risks of ineffective permissions are substantial. Unauthorized users could gain access to IT resources and wreak havoc on the applications and data. Companies could risk not meeting rigorous security and privacy compliance requirements. And the IT help desk could spend countless hours mitigating these risks.

There are typically two areas in which the IT department feels the most heat. First is in the process of how a user is provisioned (or de-provisioned) when he joins (or leaves) the organization. If the provisioning process is not automated, new hires could spend numerous unproductive hours or days waiting to get access to key applications and resources. On the other hand, if a user is not de-provisioned accurately, they could gain unauthorized access to applications and data after they leave the company, posing a serious security risk.

And that's not all. Unauthorized end users could also gain access to the company's intranet (or extranet) portal, exposing sensitive data. It is imperative that the intranet/extranet portal be able to authenticate and authorize users by leveraging user identities to eliminate unauthorized access, as well as personalize the look and feel of the portal.

So, how does one go about automating a provisioning platform and building a secure portal? Application protocols like LDAP directories lack the architectural flexibility to capture and maintain detailed information about people and complex organizational relationships. An LDAP directory could capture that Jean is a manager, for instance, but it cannot know details like her business role, whom she manages, or what applications she should have access to based on her business role. This is why the business context of a user is critical when automating provisioning or building a portal.

In this chapter, we will demonstrate how an organization can take a role-based approach to automate provisioning and personalize a portal. We will review how a reference architecture is built using portal, role manager, and provisioning tools. We will then explore how Schneider National Inc., a multinational trucking company, successfully automated employee on-boarding and personalized its intranet portal using **Oracle Role Manager (ORM)**, **Oracle Identity Manager (OIM)**, and **Oracle WebCenter**.

Reference architecture

Any organization that implements a role-based platform for automated provisioning and a personalized portal must first implement an integrated identity-management platform to manage risk, protect sensitive information assets, and improve business performance. An identity management suite can also be used to integrate information portals, providing a sophisticated solution for access management, provisioning, and role management for both provisioning and the portal.

The solution should include four key components—a provisioning platform, a role management platform, an access management platform, and a portal.

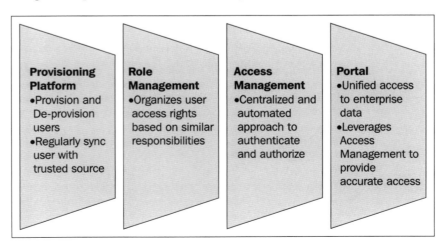

- **Provisioning platform**

  The provisioning platform pulls identities from the trusted source (often an HR system) and facilitates provisioning by automatically creating accounts on the target system. It is responsible for synchronizing user data between the HR system and target systems where there are changes to user data like new hires, job role changes, or employee termination. When the user is removed from a role and no longer requires access, the provisioning platform automatically deletes the user privileges from the target system.

  The provisioning platform extracts user attributes such as role and relationship data from Oracle Role Manager through **application programming interfaces (APIs)**. The provisioning platform maintains a comprehensive, time-stamped audit trail of all user-provisioning activities.

- **Role management**

  The importance of role-based management is a relatively new component of IAM that is quickly gaining acceptance. Based on a 2009 field research, for instance, the Burton Group highlighted the importance of role management, stating that role-based initiatives benefit a business by improving compliance and reducing risk and expenses associated with excessive privileges.

  Many organizations are adopting role-management technology to speed the provisioning process. Role management organizes user-access rights based on similar responsibilities across the enterprise. For instance, a company might formalize job codes or responsibilities into particular roles that carry their own specific system access rights and security levels. As a user's role changes, so does his/her access permissions. OIM pushes these changes to the role manager, which derives user role membership and access information based on the user profile sent from the trusted resource. The provisioning platform and role manager should work in tandem to ensure that provisioning events are based on roles.

- **Access management**

  An access management platform allows users of applications or IT systems to log in once and gain access to IT resources across the enterprise. This allows the organization to create a centralized and automated **Single sign-on (SSO)** solution for managing who has access to what information across the IT infrastructure.

- **Portal**

  Portals provide unified access to enterprise information in a personalized fashion. Portals can leverage the access-management platform to authenticate and authorize users. Once the user is authenticated and authorized, the portal presents an interface that can be personalized for each user and will display only the data and applications he has access to.

To understand how these different components work together, let's review the following architecture:

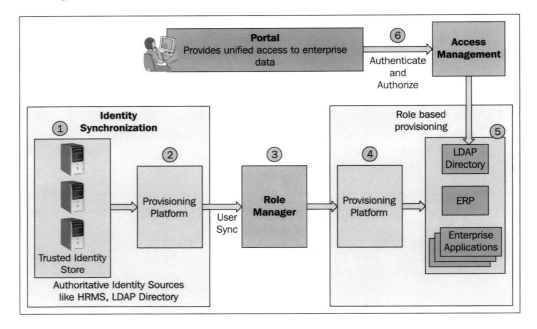

1. When a new user is created in the authoritative identity source, a notification is sent to the provisioning platform.
2. The provisioning platform provisions the user in the role manager.
3. The role manager assigns the user a hierarchy based on the user's attributes.
4. Roles, memberships, approvers, and provisioning attributes are calculated and passed back to the provisioning platform.
5. The provisioning platform creates, revokes, and modifies accounts on target enterprise applications. One of the accounts provisioned is an LDAP directory that stores user identity in groups based on their roles.
6. The access management layer uses the LDAP directory to authenticate and authorize users requesting access to the portal layer.

Now that we have seen how a reference solution works, we can examine how Schneider National Inc., a trucking company, automated employee on-boarding and personalized portal access to employees based on their roles.

Rocky road: A trucking company's outdated infrastructure

Schneider National Inc., based in Green Bay, WI, is a multinational provider of transportation services and logistics solutions that recently updated its IAM solution. The 75-year old company and its wholly owned subsidiaries employ a complex IT infrastructure that supports a range of user types, including employees, associates, customers, and vendors. Although Schneider is not a publicly traded company, internal directives require that it adhere to compliance standards like Sarbanes-Oxley.

In recent years, Schneider's homegrown provisioning solution proved unable to handle the growing compliance requirements and increasing complexity of the business environment. The existing solution could centrally manage accounts on multiple target systems, but it required considerable IT resources to manage connectivity with the target systems.

The company's on-boarding process relied on manual requests and provisioning. The solution employed a *model after* approach to requesting access for new employees. Over time, the security team discovered the system was granting more access than the user required, which put the company in danger of compliance violations.

In an effort to correct the access rights, access requests were adjusted multiple times, which complicated accurate tracking of users' access rights. The confusion led to delays in assigning access rights to new hires and internal transfers, which resulted in a loss of productivity.

Similarly, suspending access of terminated employees was a manual process that required managers to request termination. However, suspended accounts were not automatically registered in the system, which impeded the security team's efforts to provide accurate internal audits of active accounts.

Schneider's existing solution also lacked a central authorized source for user profile attributes, and the company's target systems did not automatically sync user profile attributes. Accordingly, Schneider's security team often did not know which user had access to what applications.

Lastly, Schneider struggled with inconsistent interfaces and applications for customers, truckers, and employees. The company's applications were not only dissimilar in interface, but also required a separate web browser session to run.

Schneider's solution using Oracle Identity Management and Oracle WebCenter

Schneider, with the guidance of PricewaterhouseCoopers, decided to address these deficiencies by replacing all legacy and home-grown solutions with packaged applications, part of a strategy to help reduce costs and standardize the IT infrastructure.

The company selected Oracle Identity Manager, Oracle Role Manager, Oracle Access Manager, and Oracle WebCenter for its new infrastructure. Schneider chose OIM, in particular, for its off-the-shelf connectors and ability to automatically manage accounts on various target systems.

Oracle Role Manager (ORM) has been replaced with Oracle Identity Analytics 11*g*, which is now the strategic product for role administration and role lifecycle management. Oracle Identity Analytics 11*g* contains a superset of the features in Oracle Role Manager 10*g*, but adds comprehensive support for access certification and identity audit. The combination of Oracle Identity Analytics and Oracle Identity Manager delivers a powerful, flexible solution for an enterprise identity administration and governance.

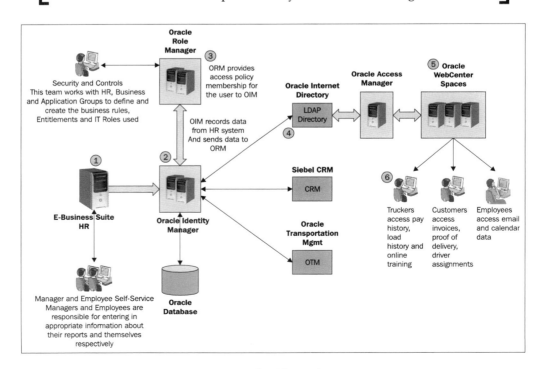

- **Oracle E-Business Suite (EBS)** HRMS is the authoritative source for user profiles. The human resources team is charged with accurately entering user-related information for existing employees in the HRMS.

- **Oracle Identity Manager**'s policy engine manages the fine-grained entitlements across managed applications, automating IT processes and enforcing security and compliance requirements like segregation of duties. It provides an automated answer to the critical compliance question of "Who has access to what, when, how, and why?". Any updates to employee information in E-Business Suite are picked up by Oracle Identity Manager and eventually provisions users in Siebel CRM, Oracle Transportation Management, and other enterprise applications.

- **Oracle Role Manager** enables business users to define user access by abstracting resources and entitlements as roles. OIM records data from the E-Business Suite HRMS system and sends data to ORM. ORM then provides access policy membership for the user to OIM. ORM acts as a supplier of role and role grant information to OIM, which in turn uses this information to provision various applications. Role grants can also be published as user attributes for LDAP directories.

- **Oracle Internet Directory (OID)** is one of the LDAP directories provisioned by OIM. OID groups are created by OIM based on ORM roles and user-role assignments.

- **Oracle Access Manager** provides an identity-management and access-control system that is shared by all enterprise applications. The result is a centralized and automated single sign-on solution for managing who has access to what information across the entire IT infrastructure. Oracle Access Manager leverages OID to authenticate and authorize users for WebCenter Spaces.

- **Oracle WebCenter Spaces** is a ready-to-use social networking application that allows business users to quickly build individual and group work environments with a few clicks. Schneider uses WebCenter Spaces to provide a collaborative environment for its employees. Users are authenticated and authorized by Oracle Access Manger.

For its consolidation platform, Schneider employed the WebLogic Oracle Server, which includes native integration for identity management components.

Because the Oracle identity management components are integrated out of the box, Schneider didn't have to build its own modules and interfaces, which saved it development costs and implementation time.

Integrating OIM with the E-Business Suite HRMS

To understand how these pieces fit together, let's review how the technology fully automates Schneider's on-boarding process for new hires.

Schneider employs the Oracle iRecruitment application for finding, recruiting, and hiring new employees. Using a self-service web interface, a job applicant creates an account and enters personal information to apply for the position. When a candidate is hired, the personal data from the application flows into the EBS system and becomes the new hire's personnel data.

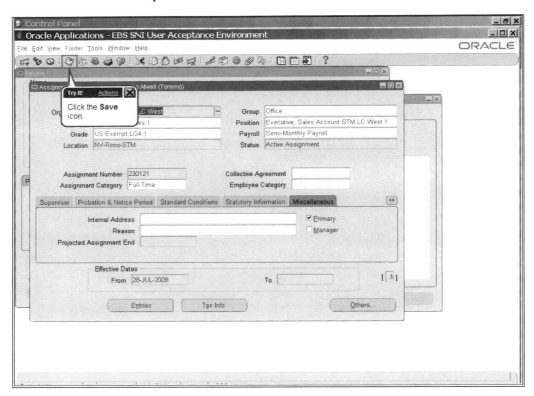

Once the employee account is created, OIM pulls user information from EBS at regular intervals to manage users on other target systems as well in its own repository. This is achieved with the EBS Employee Reconciliation Connector.

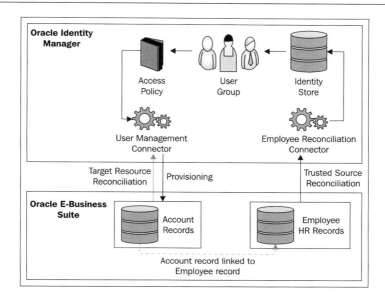

EBS Employee Reconciliation Connector retrieves employee records from the EBS HR store and creates identities from them in OIM, using a process known as trusted source reconciliation. (It uses the User Management Connector when E-Business Suite is a target resource for OIM.) For more details, visit `http://download.oracle.com/docs/cd/E11223_01/doc.910/e11202`.

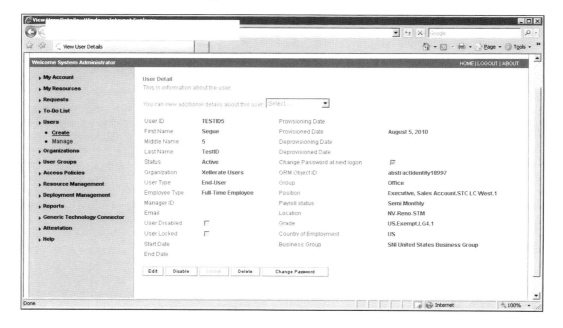

Oracle Identity Manager also uses E-Business User Manager Connector to create users on Oracle E-Business Suite and assign responsibilities based on their roles. Using EBS integration with OIM, Schneider electronically enrolled 100 percent of its employees in the annual benefit enrollment, which saved significant costs because employees did not have to print, distribute, and process paper-based forms.

In the event of employee termination, OIM uses data from the HR system to determine the employee's last day of employment. On the last working day, the OIM system automatically removes the user's access from all target systems. For forced terminations, Schneider has established an emergency team who can remove the user account directly from OIM. When user accounts are removed from OIM, OIM automatically removes all target system accounts attached to the deleted user.

Schneider also configured OIM to recertify all accounts from target applications on a regular interval. This enabled the company to detect all orphaned accounts on all target systems and override any changes made directly on the target systems. Schneider also leveraged OIM to manage and sync passwords on all target systems and employed OIM's self-service password reset functionality to provide self-service capability to end users.

Integrating OIM with ORM

ORM acts as a supplier of role and role-grant information to OIM, which in turn uses this information to provision various applications. When ORM is deployed with Oracle Identity Manager, the integration between components is bundled and preconfigured. ORM's dynamic business roles automate role membership based on job codes (such as executive, sales account) or other business relationships. Previously, role definitions were manually tracked in far-flung spreadsheets. The new system enables Schneider to manage employees across the role lifecycle in a centralized, automated repository.

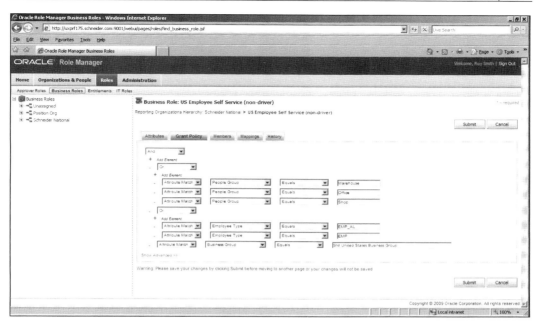

ORM derives a user's access based on role membership (**US Employee Self Service**, **(non-driver)**, as shown in the previous screenshot) and automatically generates accounts on target applications, which can dramatically speed on-boarding of new employees.

For personnel changes such as promotions or reassignments, the HR system modifies the user profile to reflect the new job and, based on role definition, ORM instructs OIM to automatically update the user's access rights and remove unneeded access privileges.

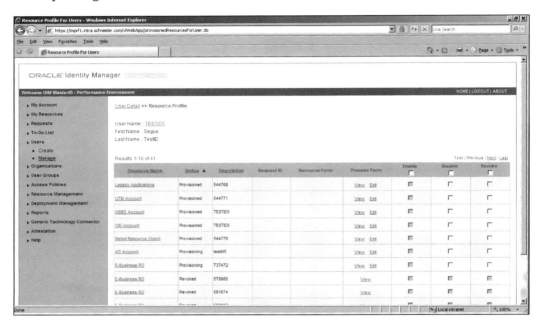

The Oracle Resource Profile within OIM creates a user profile that defines the applications that each employee can access. Using out-of-box connection tools, Schneider's IT team configured OIM to manage automatic provisioning on EBS, Siebel, Oracle Internet Directory, Microsoft Active Directory, Microsoft Exchange 2007, and Oracle Database. The company also configured OIM to manage users on other target systems by leveraging OIM's adapter factory to enable Java-based integration with other target systems.

Oracle Virtual Directory (OVD) acts as a proxy between OAM and OID and provides real-time virtual views of identity data from any data store, including directories, databases, and the Web.

Integrating WebCenter Spaces with Identity Management

Schneider used the Oracle's WebCenter Spaces module to build flexible, robust, individual and group work environments. The company employed the functionality and flexibility of WebCenter Spaces to create portals for its employees, and plans to implement portals for customers and all truck drivers next year. WebCenter Spaces has allowed Schneider to build a portal that combines various applications into one interface with a common look and feel.

In its previous solution, the company's applications were not only dissimilar in interface, but also required a separate web browser session to run. The new WebCenter employee portals require only one browser session and enable users to more quickly and efficiently complete tasks.

Each Schneider employee has access to an individual portal based on user roles that provides access to appropriate applications and data.

Based on the job responsibility assigned by the HR in EBS, ORM will assign the proper business role to the user. Using this business role, OIM will automatically create a user account on OID and assign proper group membership.

Schneider adopted OID for its ability to seamlessly integrate with other Oracle products, including OAM, Oracle Collaborative Suite, Oracle E-Business Suite, and Oracle Enterprise Manager. Schneider uses OID as a scalable directory to store identity and metadata information for OAM and WebCenter.

At Schneider, OAM authenticates users and enforces the organization's access policy through Web Agents (Oracle WebGates) installed on the WebLogic server that hosts WebCenter.

The first time a user accesses WebCenter without authentication, OAM will require the user to log in using their single sign-on credentials. After login, OAM will pull the user credentials from OID and, based on access policy, will allow or reject access to the WebCenter.

After authentication, WebCenter will present a portal to the user based on their role in the Schneider organization:

- Schneider employee portals allow users to view and respond to e-mail and calendar events from a customized portal. Schneider is also considering adding dashboards that will be provide real-time information and metrics, based on the user's role or department.

- For drivers, Schneider will build a portal that allows user access to individual information like pay history, load history, and online training.

- The customer portals will enable users to view individual data—for instance, invoices, proof-of-delivery documentation, and drivers' assignments, and perform tasks like request rate for a shipping order.

Summary

The new suite of identity management solutions enabled Schneider to achieve notable gains in efficiencies that has had a positive impact on operating costs. Using this solution, the company reduced the total time of on-boarding from several days to 24 hours. This has brought significant cost-savings and efficiencies because new hires are able to start work on day one.

OIM's ability to automatically remove terminated employees significantly improved Schneider's overall security posture, since the company no longer worries about being out of compliance due to orphaned accounts.

OAM's higher availability enables the company to run multiple instances to provide efficiency and reduce redundancy. Since implementation of the new system, Schneider has experienced less downtime due to system outages and that has boosted productivity.

The new system has also enabled Schneider to minimize manual processing of certain items. For instance, the company has streamlined payroll because it can now handle checks electronically. Similarly, 100 percent of its employees now fill out benefits enrollment online, obviating the need to mail and process paper forms.

Finally, the implementation enables Schneider to quickly generate audit reports to determine user access rights for regulatory compliance reports.

Schneider Transportation's out-of-date infrastructure couldn't keep pace with increasing demands for efficient on-boarding, identity management, certification, role-management, and data-sharing with business partners. The company implemented a scalable system based on the Oracle Identity Management Suite to standardize its technology and incorporate effective identity and access management with role-based access control. WebCenter enabled Schneider to easily create portals for employees (and soon all truckers and business partners) for streamlined and secure access to its system, resulting in a solution set that can easily mature and grow with the business.

Index

Oracle Approvals Management. *See* AME
Oracle BPEL PM integration, with Oracle
    Coherence
  about 72, 73
  coherence_config.xml, creating 77
  Coherence.jar 78
  Java implementation class, creating 75, 76
  Java objects, creating from schemas 75
  process, deploying 78
  process, verifying 78
  schema creation, for request
    and response 74
  steps 74-78
  Tangosol.jar 78
  WSDL creation, for WSDL 74
Oracle BPEL Process Manager. *See* BPEL
    PM
Oracle Business Intelligence Applications.
    See BI APPS
Oracle Business Intelligence Enterprise
    Edition. *See* OBIEE
Oracle Business Rules. *See* OBR
Oracle Business Rules Designer 58
Oracle Coherence integration, with Oracle
    BPEL PM. *See* Oracle BPEL PM
    integration, with Oracle Coherence
Oracle Data Integrator. *See* ODI
Oracle E-Business Suite. *See* EBS
Oracle Enterprise Architecture Framework.
    See OEAF
Oracle Essbase 103
Oracle Fusion Middleware 13
Oracle Identity Manager. *See* OIM
Oracle JDeveloper 48
Oracle Payables 48
Oracle Role Manager. *See* ORM
Oracle SOA Suite 49
Oracle Universal Content Management.
    See UCM
Oracle Virtual Directory. *See* OVD
Oracle WebCenter
  about 182
  Schneider's solution 186
Oracle WebCenter Spaces 49
  integrating, with Identity
    Management 193, 194

ORM
  integrating, with OIM 190, 192
  Oracle Access Manager 187
  Oracle E-Business Suite (EBS) 187
  Oracle Internet Directory (OID) 187
  Oracle Role Manager 187
  Oracle WebCenter Spaces 187
OVD 192

P

Pardee Homes
  process improvements 20
PCCM 67
PM 72
PO 155
Primary Care Case Management. *See* PCCM
process execution
  managing 39
process implementation
  about 33
  BPEL executable process, developing 34, 35
  BPMN to BPEL round-tripping 35, 36
  business services, developing 35
Process Manager. *See* PM
process modeling
  BPA Suite application 32
  case study 31
  participants 32
Property Management Reporting Solution,
    at Arcturus
  ClientConnect solution, 160
purchase orders. See PO

R

real-time BI
  building, requirements 83
  historical intelligence 82
  near-real-time intelligence 82
  need for 82
  real-time intelligence 82
real-time BI, requirements
  BAM 83
  Grid caching 84
  SOA 83
  Web 2.0 Portal 83

human interaction within Business process
    leveraging BI dashboard 132
web service access to BI insight from busi-
    ness process 132
SSO 183

T

Task List WebCenter application
    reports, delivering to property managers
    176-179
travel and expense management
    bolt-on niche application 45
    choices 44
    choices, impact 46
    code-free extensions and integrations 45
    native customization 44, 45
    solution deployment, key characteristics 46

U

UCM
    about 142
    security model 146
UCM security model 146
UniApp Framework
    about 18
    database layer 19
    enterprise data layer 19
    enterprise workflow layer 19
    principles 20
    user experience layer 19
University energy efficiency management

about 110
EMMA data mart, structure 114
EMMA OLAP, data structure 115, 116
EMMA OLTP, data structure 112, 113
EMMA roadmap 117
meter data 111, 112
OBIEE dashboards, viewing 116, 117

V

variance threshold rule
    about 167
    selecting 167

W

WebCenter security model 145
Web Services Description Language.
    See **WSDL**
Web Services Invocation Framework.
    See **WSIF**
Wind River
    about 139
    Enterprise 2.0 approach 140
WSDL 54, 170
WSIF 72

X

XML 63
XML Schema Definition. *See* **XSD**
XSL-FO 158
XSD 89

Thank you for buying
Oracle Fusion Middleware Patterns

About Packt Publishing

Packt, pronounced 'packed', published its first book "Mastering phpMyAdmin for Effective MySQL Management" in April 2004 and subsequently continued to specialize in publishing highly focused books on specific technologies and solutions.

Our books and publications share the experiences of your fellow IT professionals in adapting and customizing today's systems, applications, and frameworks. Our solution based books give you the knowledge and power to customize the software and technologies you're using to get the job done. Packt books are more specific and less general than the IT books you have seen in the past. Our unique business model allows us to bring you more focused information, giving you more of what you need to know, and less of what you don't.

Packt is a modern, yet unique publishing company, which focuses on producing quality, cutting-edge books for communities of developers, administrators, and newbies alike. For more information, please visit our website: www.packtpub.com.

About Packt Enterprise

In 2010, Packt launched two new brands, Packt Enterprise and Packt Open Source, in order to continue its focus on specialization. This book is part of the Packt Enterprise brand, home to books published on enterprise software – software created by major vendors, including (but not limited to) IBM, Microsoft and Oracle, often for use in other corporations. Its titles will offer information relevant to a range of users of this software, including administrators, developers, architects, and end users.

Writing for Packt

We welcome all inquiries from people who are interested in authoring. Book proposals should be sent to author@packtpub.com. If your book idea is still at an early stage and you would like to discuss it first before writing a formal book proposal, contact us; one of our commissioning editors will get in touch with you.

We're not just looking for published authors; if you have strong technical skills but no writing experience, our experienced editors can help you develop a writing career, or simply get some additional reward for your expertise.

Oracle SOA Suite 11*g* R1 Developer's Guide

ISBN: 978-1-849680-18-9   Paperback: 720 pages

Develop Service-Oriented Architecture Solutions with the Oracle SOA Suite

1. A hands-on, best-practice guide to using and applying the Oracle SOA Suite in the delivery of real-world SOA applications

2. Detailed coverage of the Oracle Service Bus, BPEL PM, Rules, Human Workflow, Event Delivery Network, and Business Activity Monitoring

Web 2.0 Solutions with Oracle WebCenter 11*g*

ISBN: 978-1-847195-80-7   Paperback: 412 pages

Learn WebCenter 11*g* fundamentals and develop real-world enterprise applications in an online work environment

1. Create task-oriented, rich, interactive online work environments with the help of the comprehensive Oracle WebCenter Suite 11*g*

2. Accelerate the development of Enterprise 2.0 solutions by leveraging the Oracle tools

Please check **www.PacktPub.com** for information on our titles